LESLIE LINSLEY'S
WEEKEND
DECORATING

LESLIE LINSLEY is one of this country's best authors of decorating, homestyle, and craft books. She and her husband, photographer and book producer Jon Aron, have collaborated on over forty books, including *Nantucket Style, Key West Houses, Hooked Rugs: An American Folk Art,* and *The Weekend Quilt.* A regular contributor to *Family Circle* magazine, she has also written numerous articles for *Woman's Day, Redbook, House Beautiful, Good Housekeeping,* and *First for Women.* Leslie's syndicated weekly newspaper column, "Quick Home Design," appears throughout the country. Leslie and Jon produce "Homestyle," a monthly photo/essay for the *Nantucket Journal;* and their company, Nantucket Press, packages books for national book publishers. Their home decorating design patterns are licensed through Butterick Company, Inc. Linsley and Aron divide their time between their studio on Nantucket Island where their daughter, Robby Savonen, is the design director, and Key West, Florida.

LESLIE LINSLEY'S
WEEKEND
DECORATING

1,001 Quick Home Decorating Ideas, Tips and How-To's

WARNER BOOKS

A Time Warner Company

Warner Books, Inc., 1271 Avenue of the Americas, New York, NY 10020

W A Time Warner Company

Printed in the United States of America
ISBN 0-446-39411-4
Cover design by Cathy Saksa
Book design by H. Roberts

Acknowledgments

I am very grateful to all my friends for their many suggestions that have contributed to my books, and especially to my newspaper columns "Quick Home Design" and "The Weekend Decorator," from which this book evolved. I am fortunate to count among my friends and family artists, decorators, designers, knowledgeable collectors, craftspeople, creative and handy persons, and those who are interested in home design as a hobby. Each is aware of and has an incredible sense of style. They have generously shared tips, clever ideas, inventive ways to solve decorating problems, and technical information. Many companies have provided invaluable product information for doing things better. I have not mentioned a product in this book without testing its effectiveness and learning firsthand that a project came out better because of it.

I have Anne and Robert Ferguson of Columbia Features to thank for introducing my column "The Weekend Decorator" through newspapers across the country. Thanks also to a dear friend, Sid Wood, for assigning me the "Simply Creative" pages at *First for Women* magazine and to decorating editor Cathy Olivucci for her continued support. Many of the features we worked on together contributed to this book.

I would also like to express thanks to my good friend and agent Alan Kellock, who always makes me laugh, and to my husband and partner, Jon Aron, who enables me to keep growing. Finally, I am especially grateful to Marianne Giffin Stanton, publisher of the *Nantucket Inquirer and Mirror,* for featuring my column "Quick Home Design" every week in a really fine newspaper that has been read around the world since 1821.

Contents

Introduction

This book was developed for the person with limited time who often feels all thumbs when it comes to do-it-yourself projects and needs a quick reference book for solving everyday home decorating problems in a flash. It is meant to be a potpourri for creative living. Dip in anywhere and you'll find something useful, from repairing a squeaky chair to freshening up a bedroom with no-sew pillows.

After writing more than forty books on home design and crafts, hundreds of decorating articles for the magazines, and a weekly newspaper column for more than five years, I've learned that the best design ideas are ones that can be executed in minutes and without a great deal of money. There are hundreds of ways to make your home more beautiful—quickly, easily, and inexpensively.

Almost every style—and they do change rapidly—brings with it a host of good ideas that are worth adapting. Ideas come from all different sources. I'm forever taking notes while browsing in boutiques, going through showrooms, traveling in another city or country, or thumbing through catalogs. Some of the best tips are offered by friends who pass me on the street.

A well-decorated home provides a great deal of pleasure

for its inhabitants, but many believe it takes too much time and money to achieve style. It doesn't have to. I'll show you how to perk up patio furniture cushions with a single bed sheet, create unusual curtain rods in an instant, transform an ordinary trash can into a colorful toy bin, make a small window seem larger, reseat a dining chair the easy way, give a lamp shade a new look with decorative trim, make interesting displays from everyday objects, brighten a dark paneled room without replacing the old panels. You'll learn space-stretching tricks; see how to achieve elegant but inexpensive finishing touches; find out what's "hot" in American collectables; get the inside scoop on how to make a great quilt purchase; and discover more than 100 last-minute holiday decorations that don't look it.

Chic on the cheap is the current design direction. You'll get the latest trends and tips for achieving decorating style on a shoestring. And you'll find information for time-saving shortcuts to fixing, refinishing, restoring, and refining what you already have, along with suggestions for the best products to use to get a job done right and where to find everything needed.

Walls

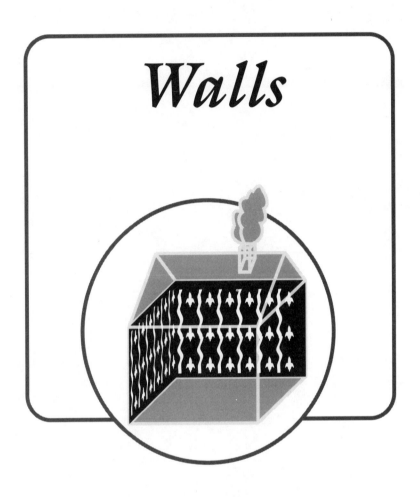

When in Doubt Paint It White

White paint will almost always make a room feel serene and calm and is the perfect background for any fabric, furniture, and paintings. Choosing the right shade of white, however, can be a problem, given the astounding range of shades available. White, while intended to be neutral, is anything but. There's rosy white with just a hint of pink. There's vanilla, achieved with a drop of yellow in the white, and linen, a pale version of vanilla. Dead white has an antiseptic quality and off-white is a little gray. Antique white comes in many different guises but most often looks like a tea bag was left overnight in the paint.

Suggestions for an All-White Room Scheme

1. Walls and carpeting gray-white.
2. Tables covered with antique-white, floor-length linens.
3. Stark white canvas-covered loveseats or sofa.
4. Linen white shades over gray-trimmed windows.
5. Add color with simple green plants in natural wood planters and an arrangement of green apples in a wooden bowl.
6. Add sparkle with fat white candles in antique gold

candlesticks, gold-framed photographs and paintings sparsely arranged.

7. Add texture with a white wool throw blanket over a sofa.
8. Add accessories such as books piled neatly here and there.

When White Shouldn't Steal the Show

All-white is the perfect decorating solution when the view outside your windows is spectacular. White provides the background for allowing the outdoors to be part of the indoors. However, an all-white house needs lots of texture to make it warm and less sterile. Use accents of natural-colored baskets, art, sculpture, sisal carpeting, and white fabric with a soft beige or textured pattern for upholstered furniture.

Unfinished wooden pieces are relatively inexpensive and can either be painted white or pickled white, that is, with patches of natural wood showing through. This approach to decorating proves that white can be very comforting and exciting at the same time.

Antidote to White

Your white rooms are a bit boring, but you don't want a major change? Create harmony in a different way with an assortment of vibrant objects such as colorful art, collections displayed appropriately, and a patchwork of Persian or Oriental scatter rugs on bare floors. Tapestry throw pillows add richness to white sofas.

A Word of Caution

When looking at paint chips, know that the color will always be much brighter on a large area. Choose a shade paler every time. And a word from the Paint Quality Institute: "Try to overestimate the amount of paint you need. If you run out before finishing the job you run the risk of not always being able to match the color exactly. Most stores will take back unopened cans or you can save the leftover for touchups."

Textured Walls

Sponging is the technique of applying one color of paint over another by dabbing it on with a sponge. It's an easy way to add rich texture to walls and a nice alternative to wallpaper. The textured walls will provide a rich background for your furniture and any printed fabric you introduce into the room. However, as with any type of craftsmanship, the results depend on the ability and care of the person applying the technique.

Quick Tips for Carefree Sponging

1. Begin by looking through a few how-to books. There are many. One that I particularly like is *Paint Magic* by Jocasta Innes (Pantheon Books).
2. Subtlety is key. The background color and the overcolor that you sponge on should be close in contrast. For example, don't use white over a color. There will be too much contrast. The background and overcolor should be just a shade apart.
3. Use a natural sponge. If you can't find a natural sponge and only have the sponge from the kitchen sink, cut

it into an irregular shape and pull pieces out of it at random to create deeper holes and crevices.

4. Practice on a piece of board.

5. Work on a small area at a time and use a light touch so you don't leave a heavy impression of paint. Go over the area, dabbing the color on so that it "feels" right. If the contrast is too stark, add some of the background color to the sponging color.

6. For interest, add a third color over the sponging color.

7. Don't get carried away and sponge everything in sight. Limit the technique to the walls and it will be most impressive. If you want to do a piece of furniture, use it in another room so that it doesn't have to fight for attention.

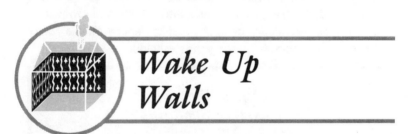

Wake Up Walls

Wallcoverings have become exciting. Patterns and textures are easier to care for and used not only on walls, but to cover doors, furniture, and ceilings and as borders around windows.

Layering

In keeping with the layered look in windows, combine techniques for wall covering. Add decoupage flowers over another floral background to create a collage of soft florals for an environment like a Vuillard painting.

Lattice Effect

Use grids to cover flowers for a lattice effect. This is a wonderful way to emphasize a particularly important area or to distort and hide architectural flaws.

Small Areas

With overlays you can introduce excitement into a small area like a bathroom. Cover walls and ceiling with wallpaper, then use some of the paper to cut out the design and apply to accessories, wastebasket, or the front of cabinets. Paper the inside of a closet door and put a few cutouts on the walls in the hallway or around door frames.

Borders

Run contrasting borders right over the wallpaper around door trims, mirrors, and windows.

Combine Paper and Paint

Paint the bottom portion of a wall, add molding or a wallpaper border for wainscoting, then apply the paper or fabric above this.

Bold Is Beautiful

Strong colors and bold patterns convey opulence. Use multiple patterning combined with rich colors for a formal environment.

Child's Room

Transform a child's room quickly, easily, and inexpensively with an imaginative wallpaper design. Use a washable, easy-to-apply paper with peel-off backing in an overall pattern, or one with scenes and murals. Cover the ceiling with star-patterned paper or one with clouds.

For Teenage Girls

Choose a delicate floral with matching fabric for a comforter. Cover lamp shades, pillows, a dresser, and a picture frame with paper or fabric to coordinate all the accessories. Paint all molding in a contrasting color. Matching roller shades are carefree for the windows.

Artful Ideas

Frame children's art or mat whimsical greeting cards or posters and paint the frames all one color. Make an arrangement and place along one wall, hanging the pictures at child's eye level. Cut out some of the wallpaper designs and apply them to dressers and chairs, around doors, or on a crib or headboard.

Stretch the Limit

Stencil designs have always been popular for decorating walls, floors, and furniture, but a repeat stencil design can be used to create a versatile border for solving all sorts of decorating problems as well. It's easy and inexpensive.

Enlarge a Small Window

Make a small window appear larger by surrounding it with a stenciled border. Apply the design to the molding or paint the molding a color, then use the same paint to stencil the wall area surrounding the window. Use the same design to stencil a border around plain curtains. Acrylic paint won't wash out of fabric.

Add Eye Appeal

If your walls lack architectural details like molding trim, add a stenciled border around the room where the walls and ceiling meet. This is less expensive and easier than putting up wallpaper.

Lower Ceiling View

A stenciled border will make a high-ceilinged bedroom more intimate. Choose paint colors to match the fabric in the room. It's easy to create your own shades of color with acrylic paint.

Create Wainscoting

The classic dining room has a molding trim or chair rail on the wall around the room. Sometimes the wall is papered above the railing or paneled under the railing. A stenciled border around the room can add interest without the expense and trouble of wallpapering, paneling, or adding chair rail molding.

Wallpaper Cover-ups

Wallpaper is a terrific solution for covering up a multitude of imperfections or ugly wall treatments. For example, if your walls are covered with thin paneling reminiscent of the fifties, you can wallpaper right over it. Prepasted paper is the only way to go.

Add Height

Striped paper makes a low-ceilinged room seem higher.

Add Warmth

Make a large, formal room more intimate by using a small, overall country pattern, or paper the top half of the walls and add rustic wood to the bottom portion. Warm colors such as sunny yellow and rosy pink add intimacy as well.

Add Space

Making a small room look big is tricky. It takes just the right combination of colors and patterns. Cool colors such as mint green, pale blues, and shades of white and beige are best. Subtle textures of pastels or white on white or beige and white stripes will expand the look. Use white or beige for the wood trim.

Faux Fakery

Faux finishes look great on walls, but if that's too much work, The Waverly Company makes a line of wallpapers with different faux-finish patterns called "Finishing Effects." There are sponge finishes, marbleizing, strié, combing, and more. They come in a range of colors. No fear of an imperfectly painted finish due to lack of talent or to interest lost halfway through the job!

For a small bedroom or bathroom try a soft peach, sponge effect. For a hallway choose a gray marbling paper.

Enlarging a Small Bedroom

Use an overall print or faux finish. Paper the inside of the closet and all doors so the room is completely finished.

Paint all the trim with a semi-gloss white paint or a shade lighter than the background color of the paper. Make wooden valances for each window and cover them with the same wallpaper. Use the background color for the curtains and keep the treatment simple.

Padded Walls

Hide ugly paneling, old wallpaper, or chipped and cracked plaster by upholstering the walls. The look is dramatic, elegant, and warm. You'll also cut down the noise level.

Quik Trak

This product, sold at home centers, makes it easy to upholster entire walls or just a small area. You don't even have to prepare the wall. All you do is staple Quik Trak to a wall, insert your fabric, and snap the track shut. The best results are achieved with lightweight fabric or sheeting to match the rest of the room. To redecorate, you simply snap in a different fabric.

Plush and Elegant

For a plush, quilted look, staple or glue cotton batting inside the Quik Trak frame (the booklet that comes with it gives directions). Then snap fabric over the batting. It looks like a million dollars. You can also buy prequilted fabric, which gives you the padding and fabric all in one.

Where to Use It

Fabric looks great on a bedroom or dining room wall. If you don't want to cover an entire bedroom, consider padded fabric on the wall behind the bed for an elegant statement. Use it in a window-seat area to match the cushion fabric.

Paint Predictions

Before painting a room you might like to know what's "hot" and what's not. I once painted my dining room bright red because it was fashionable. The following year all the magazines said white was in and a clean, fresh look was more desirable. Suddenly my red room looked like last week's dead flowers. Fashionable colors are born in the clothing industry, then emerge in interior home decoration, after which they show up on automobiles and finally become popular shades for house paints. The process takes approximately two to four years.

What Color to Choose Now?

If you want to know what color to paint your living room, look through your closet to see what colors you were wearing two years ago.

What Color Next Year?

If you think you'll be repainting a room two to four years from now, just check the current fashion catalogs to make a calculated guess about the color of the future. You might not be so inclined to choose red now if you know that yellow will be the color most likely to show up the next time around.

Choosing Color for Where You Live

The experts recommend that you choose a shade of paint that's compatible with the local environment. For example, if you live in Florida, use a bright pastel color. If you live in New England, don't. If you live in the Northeast, try shades of gray. Beige and green, barn red, Williamsburg blue, and off-white work well together in country homes.

Colors for Any Room, Anywhere

The softened, earthy desert colors of the Southwest—adobe, clay, beige—can be adapted to different parts of the country and different environments. A coral color, for example, can be softened by adding just a drop of the color to a base white to give the room a slight glow without being too shocking. In sunny environments the colors need to be more intense.

Contrast for Color Adds Punch

Since paint has to cover a large surface, you might consider adding a second color for greater visual interest. The trim around windows, doors, and wainscoting can be painted with a slightly darker shade than the walls. Highlight decorative or unusual architectural details with a third color to add "punch" and draw attention to them.

Quality Counts

Regardless of the colors you select, buy a top-quality acrylic latex paint, be it flat, satin, semi-gloss, or gloss. High-quality paints last much longer than ordinary paints.

Floors

Focus on Floors

An easy way to add texture, color, and contrast to a room is with floor covering. This expanse of space can be emphasized for a strong statement or softened to quiet a room that is otherwise busy.

Combination

Combine carpeting in some areas with vinyl flooring in others and bare floors in still others. Create the exact ambience needed for each area.

Bold and Graphic

For a small apartment, simplicity is best. Use black, white, or gray with conscious accents. Black and white 12-inch checkerboard vinyl tiles are striking in a kitchen. Use high-gloss black appliances and all-white china. A black leather sofa looks good on wall-to-wall gray carpeting. Cut flowers, art, and books are good color accents.

Vinyl Makeovers

Flexible floor coverings make for a perfect do-it-yourself project. It's a simple, instant makeover. It's easy to cut sheets of vinyl flooring and they don't even require adhesives. Moreover, you can put it right over existing floors. This is a practical way to redo a child's room, bathroom, family room, or kitchen.

Faux Tile

The richness and durability of handcrafted terra-cotta is simulated in easy-care, never-wax, quiet, foam-cushioned tile flooring. Use it in a family room or kitchen where practicality is as important as looks. Earth tones and white are wonderful for a room that has been done in neutral colors.

What's Practical?

If mildew and moisture are a problem in your home, vinyl tile is a good choice. It's often recommended for vacation homes.

Natural Elegance of Wood

Wood floors can be treated in a number of ways, such as staining, bleaching, pickling, stenciling, and combing, depending on the condition of the wood. Good floors are important to any space. If you're putting down a new floor, oak is the preferred choice.

Keep It Light

For a vacation home, light floors are best. Yellowy pine is carefree and airy. Stains in gray tones look like the silvery shingles on weather-worn exteriors. Use area rugs to allow the bare wood to show. See pickling technique on page 23.

Ceramic Tile

This is costlier than vinyl tile, but it offers a multitude of design possibilities. It's a practical and versatile choice for bathrooms and kitchens. Use tiles as a decorative element for borders around doors and windows. They can also serve as wainscoting and on parts of furniture. Create a mosaic on a table top. There are so many designs to work with.

Stenciling

This is one of the most popular techniques for enhancing painted floors and is a good way to hide a surface that has been damaged. Home centers carry the materials as well as pre-cut designs. Place the design around the floor's edge, then use rugs in the center of the room.

Combed Finish

This painted design draws attention to the floor with a wavy pattern that was popular in Early American homes. Begin with a clean floor. Apply a coat of primer, let dry, then apply a coat of paint in desired color. Let dry. Apply a dark coat of glaze or thinned oil paint (thin slightly with mineral spirits). The "comb" is made from a 6-inch-wide squeegee, notched unevenly. Comb the squeegee through the paint or glaze; the overcoat will come away, revealing the ground color in a combed pattern.

Glazed Floors

For an unusual finish, coat the floor with red casein paint. Over this add khaki color, then rub off the khaki to allow the red to show through. Wax the floor and don't worry about the wear and tear. The more it wears, the better. It just gets softer and prettier the more you walk on it.

Carpet Know-how

Your floor is often called "the fifth wall" of your home. Create an environment that is flexible, functional, and fashionable for your life-style. Selecting carpeting is an important decision because it's an investment you'll live with for a long time. When purchasing, consider the following:

Color

Performs decorating magic. It can visually alter space, camouflage or highlight architectural details, and create a special mood. Lots of color in your fabrics? A neutral carpet unifies all the elements in the room. Great architectural details? Choose carpet color to match molding trim.

Color Scheme

Borrow one of the colors from a favorite piece of fabric or a painting to create a color scheme.

Texture

A smooth, satiny, glossy surface will reflect light and make colors appear lighter, brighter, and more intense. Uneven, nubby, matte surfaces absorb light and make color appear darker and more subdued. For a casual, country setting, a highly textured carpet is perfect. Carpet with a smooth, velvety texture is more luxurious and formal.

Make a Large Room Cozy

Choose a carpet in the warm red, orange, and yellow family.

Expand a Small Room

Choose a carpet that's light in tone.

Too Much Heat

Colors such as cool green, blue, and violet help cool sunny southern and western exposures.

Defining Areas

Use broadloom area rugs. To expand space *and* define activity areas, choose different textures of carpet in the same color.

Shopping Tips

1. Living room: If you entertain frequently, stain resistance and cleanability are important.
2. Dining room: Same as above.
3. Family room: Dense carpeting with soil and stain resistance. Use patterns and multicolor tweeds.
4. Bedroom: Low-traffic areas where delicate colors and textures work. Durability may not be critical.
5. Kids' rooms: Tough, easy-to-clean. Consider medium colors with a soil-hiding pattern.
6. Kitchen and bathroom: Moisture, mildew, and stain resistance are important.

Long Live Your Carpet

Top-quality padding extends the life of your carpet and adds to its luxurious feel. Good padding is about ⅜ inch thick. Don't skimp on this item, especially under top-quality carpet. It will look better for much longer.

Paint a Checkerboard Pattern

Do you have an old linoleum floor? An unattractive wood floor? A badly stained floor? An uninteresting floor? Create an exciting new look by covering the floor with a two-color painted pattern of squares in alternating light and dark colors.

Sizes

For a large room the squares should be 12 or 14 inches. For a small area, such as a hallway, they should be about 4 inches.

Creative Color Combinations

Black and white
Forest green and white
Shaker blue and white

Preparation

Thoroughly clean the floor no matter the material. You'll need a measuring tape, graph paper, pencil or chalk, straight-edge, masking tape, paint brush, paint roller, latex or oil-base paint, and water-base acrylic varnish (non-yellowing) to seal the floor. (Polyurethane yellows the white.)

Easy Does It

Measure the area to be painted and draw to scale on graph paper. Experiment with the size of the squares. The size should divide evenly into the room measurement or you can have half squares or a border around the edge. Use a roller to paint the entire floor with white paint. Let dry. Start at the center of the room and, working outward, rule off the squares on your floor. Use masking tape to screen off the areas around every other square to be painted with the dark paint. Brush the dark paint on the exposed squares. Let dry. Remove the tape carefully so you don't pull up the white paint underneath. Coat the entire floor with water-base varnish.

Pickling Method

If you want the grain of the wood to show through, use an oil-base paint in a country color such as Shaker blue, Williamsburg green, or pale pink with white. Thin the white paint with paint thinner and roll it on lightly so it just seals the wood but allows the grain to show through. Then backtrack and wipe some of the excess paint away with a dry cloth, leaving a faint film of paint. Always go in the direction of the grain. Let dry.

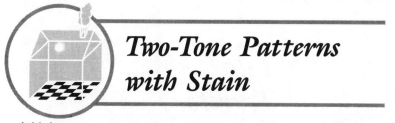

Two-Tone Patterns with Stain

Add drama to an entryway or dining room with a two-tone, wood stain border of checks or diamonds around the floor. The Minwax Company makes a product called Wood-Sheen. It's a one-step stain and polyurethane finish that comes in various wood colors such as pine, oak, and walnut and can be applied to a new floor.

Borders

First stain the floor with a light color, such as oak. Then, starting approximately 4 inches from the wall, place a strip of masking tape from wall to wall on the floor around the room. Create a grid of checks or diamonds by laying strips of ½-inch masking tape in that pattern within the 4-inch border area.

Use a sponge brush or cheesecloth to apply dark stain, such as walnut, to the unmasked areas. It should be applied lightly so the color won't bleed. Let dry. Peel away the tape. For a finishing touch use the darker color for the wall molding to frame the area.

Simulated Area Rug

For an alternative design use this method to create an area rug to look like a floor cloth. You can use any precut border stencil design. Determine the size of your area rug. Draw a rectangle on the floor and using a stain color that contrasts with the color of the floor stencil the design within the area to create the rug.

Tile Territory

Ceramic tiles are appreciated for their decorative quality, but they are also practical and functional. As a means of decoration the tile is unsurpassable for quality and purity of color, which, when dimmed by accumulated layers of grime, needs little more than a wipe of a cloth to restore its original, lustrous condition.

What Is Ceramic Tile?

It's a mixture of clays that has been shaped and fired at high temperatures. The hardened slab that results from this process may then be glazed or decorated or it may be left untreated. Ceramic tiles have been produced for centuries and there are many ancient examples of the art that attest to their timeless beauty and durability.

Italian Style

Italy is the world's largest producer and exporter of ceramic tile, with about 400 ceramic tile factories throughout the country. Most of the tile manufactured in Italy is glazed (color applied over natural clay), which affords an almost infinite variety of colors and decoration.

Sizes

The typical Italian tile measures 8 inches square. However, tile dimensions range from sizes as small as 4 inches to as large as 24 inches. Twelve-inch tiles have become the preferred size for floors. In addition to squares and rectangles, there is a wide selection of shapes, which can be used by themselves or combined with others to create an infinite variety of patterns.

Designs

Today's tiled interiors can be prettily flowered, boldly geometric, colorfully striped, or cleverly chromatic in any color imaginable.

Where to Use What

Some types of tile are suitable for particular applications while others are not. Tiles to be used outdoors, for example, must be frostproof. Unglazed tiles have greater slip resistance than glazed tiles and are best used in a hallway.

First Impressions

Create a dramatic first impression with tile in the entryway. Custom designs are endless, from a simple checkerboard to a solid expanse of colored tile with an elaborate border or inserts. Here's where bigger, brighter, bolder can be better.

From Plain to Fancy

Tile can help make up for the design limitations of the space. Depending on the design and how they are laid, tiles can expand the area. A pattern also can be designed to repeat an architectural motif in the house.

Face-Lift for a Fireplace

Surrounding a fireplace with decorative tiles was a common practice in the early 1900s, and the fireproof qualities of tile still make it a suitable facing for fireplaces and hearths. Create a border of decorative tiles to make the fireplace a focal point of the room.

Learning More About Tiles

If you're interested in learning more about the history of decorative tiles you can send for a wonderful book put out by The Italian Tile Center for the International Tile Exposition. It is located at 499 Park Avenue, New York, NY 10165.

Art Under Foot

A new or old hooked rug is the only accent needed to give a room warmth. It adds substance, texture, and color as well as being practical. Some rugs make wonderful wall decorations if they are too fragile for everyday use. Hooked rugs are more interesting than a braided or manufactured one. The most sought-after rugs are known as "storytelling." They are illustrated and reveal a simple message in a visual manner.

Traditional Style

Even if your fabrics are traditional, such as chintz florals, tapestries, or plaids, antique scatter rugs in vibrant florals or colors that go with your fabrics will mix well.

Unusual Setting

Use a hooked rug where it's least expected. The bathroom is hardly the setting most of us think of first for using a hooked rug, but this item will make an otherwise cold tiled bathroom seem homey.

Country Style

Geometric rugs with patterns similar to those found on quilts are most at home in a country setting. Use several in a long hallway or on a wood floor in a bedroom or living room. Place an interesting hooked rug over an area rug or wall-to-wall carpet. A geometric rug looks good over an Oriental or Persian carpet.

A Different Approach

Place a small rug on a rich, wooden table. It's a nice way to display a rug when the table isn't in use. Add a variety of interesting pottery on top.

Kitchen

Rugs with fruit designs will look good on a wood or tiled kitchen floor. Choose a rug with colors that match the floor. A geometric design will give a contemporary kitchen a welcoming feeling.

Windows

Window Wonders

Dressing up windows has never been easier. Anything goes. Home centers have a multitude of rods and poles designed to achieve a custom look for any style of window.

Curtain and Drapery Know-how

Windows come in all sizes, and there's a drapery or curtain for every situation. Long draperies generally create a formal effect, while short curtains look more casual. For a country-style environment use full draperies with ruffles and wide tiebacks.

Create Illusion

Curtains can create an illusion, altering the look of the window dimensions. Here are some problem-solving techniques:

Widen a Window

Extend the track beyond the window frame. This trick will also allow for maximum light when draperies are fully opened.

Reduce Window Expanse

Use tiebacks on side panels that meet at the top, then add a matching valance.

Make a Window Taller

Hang the rod a few inches above the top of the frame. If you add a valance over the extended area, the window will appear longer.

Reduce Window Height

Add a draped valance that will create a soft, elegant effect. Café curtains are a nice change for a tall window, adding lightness and airiness.

Divert Attention

To de-emphasize a rather uninteresting window or view, match the window treatment to the color of the walls so it blends in. On the other hand, sometimes it's better to use the opposite approach and bring attention to a nondescript window by exaggerating it with a lovely treatment. You could make it the focal point in the room by using a shade behind the draperies.

Accurate Measurements

When choosing a window treatment, measure all windows. Don't assume that every window in a room is the identical size.

Keeping It Simple

There are many ways to achieve a clean, simple, uncluttered window treatment without losing any of the positive decorating aspects. Vertical blinds come in a wide variety of weaves and colors that give them new dimension. Levolor, for example, sells vertical blinds in fabric as well as aluminum.

Sleek and Sophisticated

Miniblinds come in more than 200 colors as well as two-tones, so you can match them to your wall color or pick up one of the accent colors from the fabric in the room.

Wood-Slat Blinds

Horizontal wooden blinds have a tropical look and enable you to control the light as well as air circulation. They come in 2½-, 3-, and 4-inch slats. They have a wonderful "Casablanca" look. Paint the window frame white for a dramatic statement.

Custom Shades

Plain and patterned custom shades come in fresh, exciting patterns and colors as well as designs. Create your own custom look with the addition of scallops, tailored braids, tassels, pulls, or eyelet and ruffles for a softer touch.

Child's Room

Change the look of a child's room with patterned shades of bright-colored scenes, then repaint the window frames to match. Though easy to care for, the shades will set the stage for fun. Fill the room with more lively color to match the scene on the shades.

Pleated Shades

Made from fabrics that are light and pretty, they also provide temperature control. Kirsch makes insulated Verosol shades, and LouverDrape pleated shades reflect and absorb much of the sun's radiation. As a window's only covering, pleated shades add a clean, crisp look that is quite contemporary. When used as an undercurtain with another treatment, they are also practical. The easy installation makes it a snap to transform your existing window treatment with a new layered look.

Latest in Layers

Rather than using one pair of draperies, it's more stylish to use two or add curtains over a shade. If you already have miniblinds, change the total look with an overtreatment of draperies.

Multi-Design

Layering gives you options for two different window treatments and multiplies the design potential. For instance, use miniblinds in the summer, then add warmth with an overtreatment for cooler months. Or combine side panels and a full valance with a café curtain. Remove the side panels, but keep the café and valance when you want a change.

Behind the Scenes

No matter what treatment you choose, or what shape window you have, there is hardware that works effectively behind the scenes and is easy to install. The Kirsch Company has an entire collection of window treatment systems that make it easy to change your window style at whim.

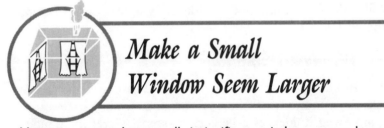

Make a Small Window Seem Larger

How can you make a small, insignificant window appear larger and more important in a room? This is a problem many of us face. The curtain and curtain rod manufacturers show us how to solve this problem by using layers of curtains that require double and triple rods. But if you have limited time and budget, here's what worked quite well for me in a guest bedroom.

Fool the Eye with Paint

Paint the window molding and sashes with a semi-gloss paint to match the wall color. White is always best when expanding the look of a small area, but if the walls are a color, you'll want the window to blend in with the walls.

Wallpaper Wisdom

Next, choose a wallpaper border with a light and airy print on a white background. Apply this around the outside of the window trim to draw the eye outward and extend the look of the window.

Let There Be Light

A lace or sheer paneled curtain will provide privacy and allow light to come through. Gather on a rod and hang from the top of the molding so the curtain extends over the trim and covers the entire window area. This will maximize the size of the window. For nighttime privacy add a plain white roller shade or miniblinds inside the window casing behind the curtain.

Window Trimmings

Emphasize the window with a dressy treatment that takes a minimum of effort. A product from Kirsch called Tulip Swag holders is a behind-the-scenes secret for pouffed swag valances, rosettes, and bishop sleeve curtains. The sewing you have to do is limited to hemming fabric panels, and the technique is similar to that of forming gift bows. In minutes you can form the fabric into rosettes, poufs, bows, hearts, shells, etc. Step-by-step instructions are packed with the swag holders, which are found in curtain departments. Hang the rod at the very top of the window molding and let it extend slightly beyond each side. This will make the window seem larger all around. Use a fabric to match the wallpaper or bedspread.

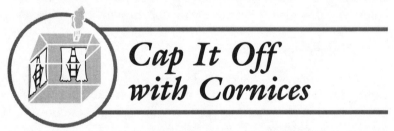

Cap It Off with Cornices

A cornice creates a finished look over a window. You can then add curtains, side panels, cafés, a shade or miniblinds. Or, if you don't want curtains, just use a cornice alone. It won't block out light.

Use 8-inch-wide pine. Measure the width of your window all the way to the edge of the molding trim and cut the wood to this measure. Then cut two pieces for the two 3- by 8-inch sides. Use Elmer's glue and 1½-inch brads to glue and nail the long piece to the long edge of each side piece. Let the boards dry overnight before working with the cornice. Your decorating choices are numerous.

Perfectly Painted

Paint the wood to match the window trim or pick up one of the colors in your curtains.

Padding Around

For an upholstered finish, cover the wood first with quilt batting, then with fabric to match your curtains or slipcovers. Cut quilt batting and fabric pieces large enough to wrap around the cornice and staple to the inside.

Paper Proud

For a coordinated window treatment, cover the cornice with wallpaper to match the room. Or paint the cornice and then add a pretty, contrasting wallpaper border. *Tip:* When ready to paste in position, center the strip of paper on the front of the cornice and press in place. Do not press the side pieces to the wood. Position the cornice over the window molding and nail with brads at each side. Then smooth the remaining paper to the sides over the nails on each side of the wood.

Faux Fabulous

A faux finish such as marbleizing or sponging is a handsome touch. You don't have to take a course in faux finishing. You'll find kits in home centers and craft shops to make a small job like this very easy and virtually foolproof. In particular, I've had success with the marbleizing kit made by Plaid. It comes in many colors.

When in Doubt, Sponge It

For a quick and easy faux finish, apply a coat of white latex paint over the wood. After it's dry, dip a natural sponge or sponge brush into acrylic paint in a soft pastel or beige and dab or swirl over the entire area.

Stencil Savvy

Apply a coat of base paint, then use a contrasting color to stencil a repeat border design across the cornice. For a child's room, choose a simple, whimsical design and use bright colors. For a sunroom choose a graceful curving vine. For a bedroom, trace a flower from your fabric or wallpaper and cut a stencil for a repeat matching pattern.

Decoupage

Cut out flowers from wallpaper or wrapping paper and arrange across the painted cornice. Use white craft glue to secure in position. This is a good way to design cornices to match the wallpaper if you are papering the wall at the same time. You can also use cut-out fabric for this project, but be sure to use very sharp scissors so the fabric edges don't fray.

Creative Ways with Curtain Rods

Change the look of a room in an instant with unconventional curtain rods.

Staked Out

Plastic plant stakes and bamboo poles are thin enough in diameter to weave through a delicate fabric or a narrow channel on a curtain. The dark green or natural colors are appealing. Select the size and thickness to suit your curtains and window and simply hang as you would a regular rod. If they are too long, it's easy to cut off the ends with a regular saw.

Nature's Way

All it takes is a walk outdoors to come up with a curtain rod that is not only different but looks great. Use a fat branch, bark and all. Look for one that is the size and thickness to suit your curtains/window. A slightly twisted and burly one will have a wonderfully rustic look. The contrast of this pole with a delicate lace curtain is interesting.

The branch can extend beyond the window on either side or can be cut to window size. Choose curtain rod brackets or large hooks in an appropriate size to hold the branch at each side of the window frame. To hold the curtain to the rod, pin or stitch evenly spaced ribbons to the top of your curtain and tie to the branch. As an added touch, weave a vine of artificial ivy around the branch to bring in more of the outdoors.

Fishing for Compliments

For a seafaring theme in a den or boy's room, use either a fishing pole or a boat paddle.

Forging Ahead

Wrought iron or forged poles used for hanging plant hooks make unusual curtain holders. These are found in garden shops and through mail order catalogs.

Country Cousins

For a simple change of pace, hang bunches of dried flowers at the edges of each standard curtain rod. Lavender wreaths make sweet curtain tiebacks.

No-Sew Curtains

For all you "all-thumbs" decorators, try the no-sew approach for a window treatment. There are lots of ways to create instant curtains without cutting or stitching.

Dishtowels Not for Drying

Dishtowels are perfect for café curtains and a valance that you can hang in ten minutes. The patterns are perky in red or blue and white checks for a crisp country feeling. The fabric has enough weight to give the curtains body and they look especially good on kitchen windows.

What to Buy

You'll need the following for a set of curtains: two tension rods to fit your window, three matching linen dishtowels (two for the curtains and one for the valance), and a package of clip-on café curtain rings.

Putting It All Together

Clip the rings evenly spaced across one end of each of two dishtowels and put them on the rod for the bottom half of the window. Turn the third towel lengthwise and drape over the top rod to create a valance. The curtains and valance will be finished on both sides, so the window will look just as good from the outside as inside. Nothing could be simpler. When you get tired of them, take the curtains and valance down and use as dishtowels.

For Larger Windows

If your windows are too large to use the towels as is, consider buying the toweling by the yard. It's inexpensive and comes 18 inches wide, finished on both edges. The only sewing required is a hem at top and bottom.

Not for Tables Only

For another inexpensive no-sew idea, make a pretty hanging valance from a square lace tablecloth. The light will shine through. Turn the cloth on the diagonal and fold in half. Hang it evenly over the rod so the corner hangs down in the center of the window. If there is excess fabric at each end, fold each corner edge back over itself to finish the sides.

Racy Lacy

And if you like the idea of lacy valances or curtains, many fabric shops sell prefinished lace by the yard in different widths. They are perfect for creating lace panels in a variety of pretty patterns for any size curtain. Simply thread them onto the rod.

Furniture

Arranging It All

Whenever the weather shifts slightly in temperature, I rearrange the furniture. I'm convinced there has to be one more way to place my sofa and chairs that I haven't yet discovered. It's great if you can find a cozy arrangement for winter, then rearrange in a looser, more open way for warmer days.

Finding a Focal Point

Arrange furniture around a fireplace or a window that faces a view. If you don't have a particularly interesting area in the room, create one. A wonderful piece of sculpture on a table, a great painting, or a grouping of framed photographs might be all it takes.

Create a Flow

The Home Furnishings Council suggests creating "lanes" to define separate areas. A sofa and two chairs around a coffee table, for example, create a conversation area. If you have another activity area, you want to be sure the flow from one to the other is accessible. They suggest a 2-foot-wide lane and an extra foot of open space for an entrance door. If you have to hurdle a sofa to get to a door you've got to rearrange.

Balancing Act

Large- and small-scale furniture works well if it's used well together. Don't place all the heavy furniture together. By the same token, vary the heights of each element. Keep large pieces against the wall. A large armoire can balance a low seating arrangement or two chairs and a table. Two armchairs with a small table between them balance a sofa.

Get-Together

Imagine how your room will be used. If you have small, intimate gatherings, two loveseats opposite each other with a coffee table between might be just right. I usually have six people when I have company and arrange my furniture for easy conversation from one side of the room to the other.

Right at Hand

A table should be within easy access and at the right height for the chair or sofa next to it.

Making Room

Furniture can do double duty in a small room. Select a tea table rather than a coffee table. It's a bit higher but doesn't look awkward, and it's fine for dining as well. A glass-top table will seem to take up less room than one that is wood. In this way you can opt for a larger surface without having it dominate the space.

Unify with Color and Patterns

Use some of the same color from room to room. Use the fabric from the sofa to cover an occasional chair in order to unify the room. Use the fabric from the sofa to make pillows for chairs in another room. The whole house will look well coordinated.

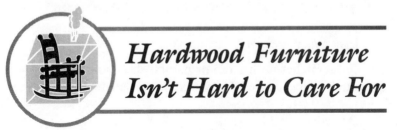

Hardwood Furniture Isn't Hard to Care For

Good furniture is built to last a lifetime. If you have good hardwood pieces, protecting and enhancing the natural beauty is surprisingly simple.

Cleaning Tips

1. Dust with a soft cloth in the direction of the grain of the wood. Use old T-shirts, baby diapers, or pieces of cheesecloth that have been washed to remove the sizing.
2. Use a mild, non-alkaline soap and water on a sponge to clean the surface. Wipe dry.
3. Use a paste wax every 6 to 12 months. Remove old wax first with a mild solution of soap and water.

Repairing Scratches and Nicks the Easy Way

Dark Wood or Stain

Fill scratches with shoe polish that matches the light shade of the finish. An alternative is to rub the area with a child's crayon or felt-tipped marker.

Cherry

Fill scratches with cordovan shoe polish or a shade of reddish brown that matches the wood. Or apply darkened iodine with a cotton swab or thin artist's brush.

Light Wood or Stain

Fill scratches with a tan or natural shoe polish, or apply darkened iodine diluted 50 percent with denatured alcohol.

Oil Finishes

Rub in the direction of the grain with a fine (000) steel wool dipped in lightweight mineral oil, paraffin oil, or boiled linseed oil. Wipe dry with a clean cloth and buff lightly.

Removing Common Furniture Stains

Water Marks and Rings

Rings are often in the wax, not the finish. Cover the stain with a clean thick blotter, press down with a warm iron. Repeat if needed. Or rub with salad oil, mayonnaise, or white toothpaste. Wipe area dry and wax or polish (also see page 61).

White Marks

Rub with a cloth dipped in a mixture of cigarette ashes and lemon juice or salad oil. Or rub with a cloth dipped in lighter fluid, followed by a mixture of rottenstone (polishing material available in hardware stores) and salad oil. Wipe dry and wax or polish.

Milk or Alcohol

Use fingers to rub liquid or paste wax into stain. Or rub in paste or boiled linseed oil and rottenstone with the grain, substituting pumice for dull finishes. Or rub with ammonia on a dampened cloth. Wipe dry and wax or polish.

Cigarette Burns

Rub with scratch-concealing polish. (See page 61 for more suggestions.)

Heat Marks

Rub a tiny area gently along the grain using a dry steel wool soap pad, or gently with extra-fine (0000) steel wool. Wipe and wax.

Nail Polish Marks

Blot the spill immediately, then rub with fine steel wool dipped in wax. Wipe dry and wax.

Paint Marks

If fresh, remove latex paint with water. Remove oil-base paint with mineral spirits. If dry, soak spot in linseed oil, wait until paint softens, and lift carefully with a putty knife. Remove residue with a paste of linseed oil and rottenstone. Wipe dry and wax.

Wax or Gum

Harden the substance by holding an ice cube wrapped in cloth against it, then use fingernail or credit card to remove. Rub area with extra-fine steel wool dipped in mineral spirits. Wipe dry and wax.

Sitting Pretty

It's easy to update dining chairs with new seat fabric. Even if the chairs are mismatched, but are well proportioned, they will look good together with the same fabric covering. The only tools you'll need are a screwdriver and staple gun (or hammer and tacks). Choose a pretty, stain-resistant fabric. A new piece of quilt batting or foam cut to size and placed under the fabric will add "oomph" to the seat. If the paint on the chair frame needs a touch-up, do it before reseating.

1. Turn the chair upside down and remove the screws from all four corners of the seat. The seat will easily come off.
2. Cut the quilt batting and fabric 3 inches larger than the seat all around. If using foam, make a seat pattern from a paper bag or large piece of Kraft paper and cut foam to exact size to fit the seat.
3. Center the quilt batting and fabric over the seat, turn the whole thing upside down and staple or tack the fabric to the underside. Make sure the fabric is stretched taut and corners are pulled evenly. Trim excess fabric from the corners.
4. Set the seat back in position on the chair and replace the corner screws, right through the fabric and batting, from the underside.

Flea Market Finds

Flea markets are a terrific way to find bargains. Some things are easily fixable, made over, covered, or recycled in an up-to-date way. I am always attracted to delicate chairs that look pretty but are uncomfortable! There's a way to fix almost any kind of furniture problem if you love the piece enough to do it yourself or spend the money to have it done. You might like to know what's in store for you in order to make this evaluation before buying.

Caning Seats

I recently found some wonderful wooden dining chairs with broken cane seats only to discover how easy it is to get them recaned or do it myself. There are caning kits on the market that make the job a cinch. Or look in the Yellow Pages for a good caner in your area. For caning materials, write to: The H. H. Perkins Company, 10 South Bradley Road, Woodbridge, CT 06525. They have a catalog.

Stripping the Finish

Almost any finish can be stripped away to reveal the naked wood beneath. If you're planning to paint the object, the old finish doesn't have to be stripped. Just sand and apply the paint. If you are planning to restain the wood, however, or restore it to its natural appearance, remove the old finish completely with an all-purpose paint remover. Formby's Wood Care Products offer complete kits for safely removing any type of wood finish without damaging the furniture.

Unwarping

The most common problem with furniture that has been discarded or left in a damp basement is warping. It can be fixed! Begin by stripping off the old finish, then sand the surface and place the warped object convex side down. Pour boiling water on the concave side. When it's well soaked, turn the warped piece over and place it in the sun. As the curved side dries, the piece will flatten out. This can take from a few hours to a few days depending on the extent of the warping. Once the piece is unwarped, bring it indoors and let it dry thoroughly. Coat both sides with shellac or varnish to keep it from absorbing moisture and warping again.

If you can't work outdoors, devise a way to prop the warped object a few inches above a radiator and place several wet rags on top of the piece. Keep the rags wet with boiling water. A furnace or hot air ducts will substitute for a radiator.

Loose Veneer

You may find a perfectly good piece of furniture with loose veneer. This is another fixable problem. Wrap a piece of 3M Press N' Sand self-adhesive sandpaper around the end of a cooking spatula. Wet it slightly and slide it under the lifted veneer. Sand back and forth to remove old glue.

Next, apply Elmer's Carpenter's Wood Glue to the object surface and the underside of the lifted veneer. Clamp and weight down the repair with heavy books. Leave to dry overnight.

Slipcover Savvy

Slipcovers solve a multitude of problems. First of all, they can cover up outmoded upholstery fabric. Slipcovers made with new decorator fabric instantly transform an old piece of furniture for today's fashion. Further, they unify a room. If the same fabric is used on all pieces, the oddball chair is pulled together with the rest of the furniture. Slipcovers also enable you to change the look for summer and winter. And finally, slipcovers are less expensive than new furniture. There are fine workrooms and stitchers who can do the job for you. Check with your local sewing center or in the Yellow Pages.

The Right Fabric

When choosing fabric, keep in mind that medium weight works best. It is durable but is easier to sew than a heavyweight fabric. Chintz is cool to the touch, especially good for summer, and is often recommended for slipcovers.

Choosing a Pattern

Florals are easy to live with and will always be stylish. Even if the fabric fades, a floral print gives the furniture a look of having a past, as if the furniture were inherited from a great-aunt.

Calm and Cool

Textured white or beige is refreshing and calms a room. Neutrals provide the perfect background for any color you might introduce. Stripes stand up to the test of time. You can use floral or tapestry pillows effectively with stripes.

Sew It Yourself

For anyone vaguely familiar with sewing techniques, it's not that difficult to make your own slipcovers. In their book *Decorating with Fabric* (Clarkson N. Potter, Inc.), Donna Land and Lucretia Robertson give clear and simple directions for measuring and making slipcovers for any piece of furniture. Or look for Butterick patterns in sewing centers.

Trying It Out

Loosely fit slipcovers that are more draped than fitted have a casual charm. Wrapping cushions and tucking here and there can actually simulate a slipcovered sofa if you want to try a fabric for a while to see how you like it.

Furniture Update with a Sponge

Sponge glazing is a painting technique that will instantly transform even the worst-looking piece of furniture. The paint mixture is applied with dabs and swirls of a sponge to achieve an overall design in the color of your choice.

Easy Does It

Begin by sanding your furniture until it is smooth to the touch. Apply a base coat of flat white enamel paint. To make the glaze, mix one ounce of turpentine with half as much boiled linseed oil and one teaspoonful of oil paint. Add to this a drop of Japan drier. (All of the materials are available in art or hardware stores.) The solution will be thin and semitransparent.

Dip 'n' Dab

Dip a small, dry sponge into the mixture and dab the color onto one small area at a time, making swirls in the glaze. To add more interest you can also use your fingers to create patterns in the glaze. When you are pleased with the overall effect, let dry for twenty-four hours.

Protecting It All

Once the glaze is completely dry, apply a coat of clear, high-gloss varnish to all exposed areas. This protects the finish and gives it a shiny glow. And you might like to know, this technique works on walls as well (just leave out the last step, varnishing).

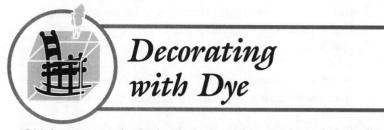

Decorating with Dye

Old furniture, unfinished wood, or wicker can be refurbished instantly to look like treasured country classics. Fabric dye is an inexpensive and easy way to stain furniture a wonderful country color like the faded blue or red found on Early American milk-painted pieces. Since the dye is transparent the wood grain shows through. Give a hand-rubbed look to kitchen chairs, a dining table, an armoire, or a coffee table. Once you've applied the color you can add a decoration such as a stenciled design in another color.

Tips for Dye Staining

1. Whenever possible, use unfinished wood or wicker.
2. If you are dyeing an old piece of furniture, completely strip away all paint, varnish, or other finish.
3. Sand the surface of the wood until smooth and wipe clean.
4. Pine, oak, walnut, cherry, and balsa all absorb the dye beautifully. Pine shows the truest stain colors.
5. To make the wood more absorbent, wet the entire piece with a water-soaked sponge before applying the stain.
6. Mix 1 part hot water to 2 parts liquid dye. Test the color by applying it with a sponge brush to a hidden area (such as the back or underside).
7. Use rubber gloves and brush the stain in one direction onto the wood. Cover all surfaces and let the stain dry to see the true color before deciding if the piece needs another coat. The dye will dry almost instantly. For best results keep the dye hot while you work.
   Note: If the wood is soft and quite absorbent, it may require several coats to achieve the desired results.
8. To finish the piece, apply a thin coat of satin varnish or polyurethane to all exposed surfaces. (If you are planning to add a stencil design, do so before varnishing.) Let dry and apply a coat of clear furniture wax for a fine sheen.

To Stencil

There are many precut stencils available in hardware stores and craft shops. Choose a color that contrasts with your background for the stencil stain; it can be lighter or darker. I especially like Rit Dye's Scarlet Red and Royal Blue on wood furniture.

1. Mix a solution of 2 parts dye and 1 part boiling water.
2. Tape the stencil in place on your furniture and dab the dye onto the cutout area with a clean sponge brush or wadded piece of paper toweling. Use a new stencil for each new color.

Since the dye is not opaque, the color behind the stencil will show through, giving it a faded appearance. This is in keeping with the country look and your piece will at once add character to any room.

For more information on decorating with dye, send for a free, fully illustrated booklet to Rit Consumer Services, Dept. DDC, P.O. Box 21070, Indianapolis, IN 46221.

Fantasy Furniture

Ready-to-finish furniture is quite affordable and it's easy to decorate with paint, stain, faux finishing techniques, and other quick and easy crafting tricks.

Multicolored High Chair

Give a high chair a spirited look by painting each of the rungs and spokes a different color. Use shades of pastels for a soft look, or combine primary colors for a bright chair. First apply a primer coat of white. Then paint each rung, spoke, or leg in a different color. Next, paint the high chair tray one color and the trim another color. Add a stencil design of random circles, squares, and triangles. Cut the shapes from a hard sponge. Press each shape onto one of the paint colors and press over the high chair tray as if you were rubber-stamping it.

Country Jelly Cabinet

An old-fashioned jelly cabinet is a versatile storage unit. It's handy for files, books, linens, or extra dishes and glassware. It's also great for storing sewing supplies. Decorate the front panels with a simple illustration. First paint the top and sides. Next, use a dark pencil to trace a design or illustration from a book or other source that will fit on the front. Tape the tracing face down on the cabinet and retrace on the back of the lines to transfer the design. Remove the tracing and fill in the outlines with acrylic paint colors of your choice.

Spatter Paint Kitchen Chairs

Give plain, wooden kitchen chairs character with a spatter-paint finish. First use semi-gloss latex to paint the chair in the color of your choice. Then dip a toothbrush into a contrasting color and run your finger over the bristles to spritz the paint over the entire surface of the chair. You can do this over and over with many different colors for a multicolored effect.

Chair Wrap

Cut out designs from pretty wrapping paper and glue them at random on the painted chair. Three coats of polyurethane protects it all. It's an easy way to make an ordinary chair fanciful.

Divider Screen

Combine a background of a faux finish with pretty floral greeting cards on the panels of a divider screen. First paint the screen with a background color, then add an overall faux technique of sponging, combing, or strié. Glue the cards to the center of each panel and frame each one with a narrow strip of velvet ribbon in a color to match each flower.

Distressing Facts

Paint an unfinished armoire a country color. Then give it an old and distressed look with antiquing. Finally, remove some of the paint by rubbing the surface down with fine sandpaper, and then steel wool, so that the wood shows through. This is a good way to create a worn, country look from a new piece of furniture. Satin polyurethane protects the furniture with a matte sheen.

Covered with Roses

Paint a small, occasional table a pale shade of pink. With a light pencil, create a 1-inch diamond grid on the diagonal over the table top. Dip an artist's brush in green paint and go over the grid lines freehand to make graceful weaving vines. Apply rose decals evenly spaced on both sides of the vines for a rose-covered trellis.

Blanket Chest

Apply a light wood stain, such as Formby's Maple Wiping Stain, to the sides of a blanket chest. For contrast, stain the lid with a darker stain such as antique walnut. Apply semi-gloss polyurethane and let dry. Dip fine black sandpaper in sudsy water and rub lightly over the entire surface. Wipe clean and the finish will be satin-smooth. A coating of bowling alley paste wax, such as Johnson's or Butcher's, will give the piece a beautiful sheen and the chest will look like expensive furniture. Or simply rub with Formby's Tung Oil Finish.

Decorative Touches with Stencils

Paint or stain a plain table, then add a stencil border around the edge. A geometric design in a contrasting color or darker stain is perfect for a square or rectangular surface. A delicate border of vines and heart-shaped leaves will give a Scandinavian flair to the door frame of a china cabinet. Use a floral border on the front of dresser drawers or on the top of a night table.

Attic Finds

Restoring old furniture can be fun as well as rewarding. Although saving money is often the motivating factor, there are other benefits to buying older furniture. According to Homer Formby, America's leading expert on wood care and refinishing, furniture that's 50 years old or older is usually made of choice wood, with more craftsmanship and care than you see in furniture made today.

Is It Worth the Effort?

How do you know if a piece of furniture is worth restoring or if, in fact, it can be restored without becoming a major project? Examine an area that isn't covered with layers of old finish. If the wood's grain looks good and the piece is sound, it's probably worth restoring.

Does It Need Refinishing?

Not all old pieces demand refinishing. Many are just dull, dirty, or tired-looking and simply need a face-lift. Use a good furniture cleaner, not a polish, and apply to the dirtiest spot on the piece. If the spot comes clean and the wood grain is clear, you won't have to restore it at all.

To Remove or Not to Remove

Formby says most people make the mistake of using paint remover when it isn't necessary. Old varnish, lacquer, or shellac finishes need only be dissolved with a furniture refinisher. (Don't make the mistake of using an all-purpose stripper. They're harsh and can strip the beautiful color from the wood.) Use a paint remover for painted or polyurethane finishes, but don't try to remove the paint before the remover can do its job. Never apply paint or other finishes in damp weather.

Solutions to Most Common Problems

Q. How can I remove water rings?
A. Squeeze white toothpaste on a damp cotton cloth and buff lightly into the ring for luster. For stubborn rings, mix toothpaste with baking soda and apply to the area.

Q. How can I repair cigarette burns?
A. Dip a cotton swab into a bottle of nail polish remover and lightly rub across the burn. It will dissolve. Then scrape any black residue with a plastic credit card. If a hollow is left, mix equal parts of clear nail polish and remover and fill in the hollow.

Q. How do I identify the finish on my furniture in order to remove it properly?

A. Touch a spot of the finish with a cotton ball dampened with nail polish remover. If the cotton sticks or softens the finish, it's varnish, lacquer, or shellac. If there's no effect, it's polyurethane.

Q. How can I remove the finish from carvings and other intricate areas?

A. Rub furniture refinisher into the area with a paint brush, with bristles trimmed to a stubby length. Or use a genuine brass brush. This will stand up to chemicals and won't scratch the wood.

Q. How do I choose the best paint remover?

A. The heavier the can, the more effective the product. Shake the can to be sure it's not thin and runny.

Q. Once the old finish is removed how do I protect the wood?

A. Apply a protective coating of tung oil, varnish, or polyurethane. Look for finishes that can be hand rubbed for a finish that will last and look naturally beautiful.

If you have any questions about refinishing you can call 1-800-FORMBYS seven days a week for free, expert advice. Hours are Monday–Friday, noon–8 P.M.; Saturday and Sunday, 10 A.M.–6 P.M. Eastern time. It's a toll-free help line that answers 70,000 questions a year on everything from dusting the coffee table to refinishing pianos.

Chair Repair

Two middle-aged women were sizing up the wares at a street fair. One advised the other, "Never buy an antique chair. Buy anything else antique, but never a chair. They're always rickety and it's impossible to get them fixed." Her friend protested, "But I thought a good restorer can glue a chair so it won't wobble." "Never!" she adamantly replied. "Eventually they all loosen and become unusable. It simply isn't worth the time, effort, and expense." Not to be deterred, her friend argued, "But all your dining room chairs are antiques." And without hesitation the other woman quickly pointed out, "That's different! Do you know how hard it is to find six matching chairs?"

Most furniture experts would advise, "Don't buy a wobbly chair, but if you find six you'd better know a good furniture restorer." A good restorer will be able to reglue a chair without taking the dowels apart. If you want to give it a try, Chair Loc is a glue for repairing loose joints and dowels. When you squeeze it on the areas the wood swells and becomes tight. Furniture makers' hot glue is best for repairs like cracks or broken dowels. This requires tying and clamping the chair to hold it together while it dries.

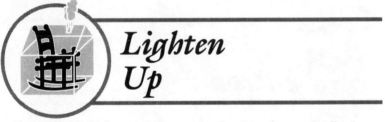

Lighten Up

If you're tired of your dark wooden furniture but can't afford new pieces, it's easy to lighten what you have.

Finish Remover Tips

Removal of old finishes may require a liquid stripper, available at most paint or hardware stores. Remove hardware from doors and drawers, and cover up areas not to be stripped. Always wear rubber gloves and work in a well-ventilated area.

Hard-to-Reach Places

Using a wire brush helps to remove old finishes from hard-to-reach areas and open-grain woods.

Bleaching

To restore the natural color of wood turned dark by age, mix equal amounts of household bleach and water. Apply this to the wood until the desired color is restored. After bleaching, rinse the wood surface with plain water and allow to dry thoroughly.

Finished Naturally

Be sure the wood is dry and smoothly sanded before applying a finish. Watco Danish Oil Finish gives a natural, hand-rubbed look and penetrates deeply into the wood pores to protect the furniture. No refinishing and no resanding are required. This finish comes in natural and light colors such as golden oak, light walnut, and fruitwood.

In a Pickle

Pickling is a good way to conceal the natural yellow tint of new pine. This look can be achieved with wood stains that come in a variety of tinted pastel shades. For a do-it-yourself solution, mix thin white enamel paint slightly with mineral spirits and brush it on raw wood. Immediately wipe it off with a clean cloth, leaving a white glaze over the entire surface (see page 23).

The Naked Truth

If you find that your piece, once stripped, has a warm, soft color, the kind that mellows with age, rub the surface with very fine steel wool, then coat with furniture paste wax. Let dry and buff for a soft sheen.

Baskets and Wicker

Bleaching or pickling lightens baskets and wicker as well. To lighten a dark pine basket, for example, simply soak for 15 minutes in a solution of equal parts household bleach and water. Baskets of willow or vines take on a new look when bleached, and you might also try bleaching pinecones for an arrangement.

Paper Patchwork Furniture

Quiltmaking has become very popular, and patchwork quilts are often found in country homes. The Early American patterns are easy to copy because most are made up of squares and triangles. Although they traditionally were created by stitching fabric pieces together, these folk designs can be reproduced by cutting the pieces from a variety of colorful, patterned wallpaper and gluing them to furniture. It's an interesting way to cover an old or ready-to-finish blanket chest.

Blanket Chest

A blanket chest is the ideal project for this technique because it has square, flat surfaces. When it is finished, you will be surprised at how much the object looks as if it were covered with fabric patches. However, no sewing is required, only accurate cutting.

Favorite Patterns

A star pattern is the most popular and there are many variations from which to choose. The Log Cabin is made of squares and rectangles and is an easy geometric design to create. Irish Chain is another popular quilt pattern that is made up entirely of squares, usually just two colors, such as white and blue.

Materials Needed

You will need: a variety of wallpaper sheets (a discontinued sample book can be obtained from a local wallcovering store), white glue, a craft knife, a straightedge, heavy paper such as a manila folder, tracing paper, a pencil, tape, spray varnish, a sponge, and a quilt pattern.

How to Do It

Trace the quilt pattern pieces and transfer them to heavy paper. Cut out these shapes to use as templates for cutting the paper pieces.

Follow the directions for making the quilt, but rather than cutting the pieces from fabric, you will cut them from wallpaper with the craft knife and straightedge. Most fabric measurements include a ¼-inch seam allowance, which you will not need.

Spread glue on the back of each paper pattern piece and build your quilt blocks according to the quilt directions. Press each piece down firmly on the chest and with a damp sponge wipe away any excess glue that may ooze out from the edges. Since your blanket chest is smaller and a different shape than a quilt, you will adjust the design accordingly. Coat the entire piece with spray varnish or brush on a coat of clear, satin polyurethane. Let dry thoroughly.

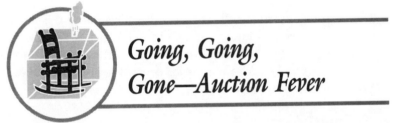

Going, Going, Gone—Auction Fever

Auctions have become a natural means of recycling furniture and bric-a-brac in my community, and I have caught auction fever. For years I've been able to furnish my home relatively inexpensively, and I have discovered some interesting pieces that I might not have been able to afford at their original prices.

Chairs

This is a good place to shop for any style, size, or type you might need. Most are in good condition and now that I've amassed more than are needed to fill an auditorium I don't mind letting you in on this little secret. However, I am a real sucker for baby-size chairs. There is always at least one small chair at every auction. Sometimes my husband and I accidentally bid against one another, which is the reason we now have four different sets of chairs in our basement. Try to sit together!

Glasses and Chinaware

There seems to be a never-ending supply of glasses and dishes, soup tureens and commodes at every auction. Always go to the preview so you don't bid on something you think is perfect only to find it is chipped or cracked.

Quilts

You might think that quilts are rare in this country. Not true; and the prices are still reasonable. It doesn't seem to matter whether they're new or old, all the quilts at every auction are gobbled up. It's often difficult to know the date of a quilt unless you know what to look for, but if it doesn't matter to you, decide which one you like and how much it's worth to you and stick to your price or let it go by. (See pages 188–90 for how to buy a quilt.)

Small Gems

Vases, silverware, baskets, jewelry, and other small gems easily transported go for large sums. If you have your heart set on something in this category, pray that your item comes up at the very end of the sale, when most of the bidders have gone home.

Large Pieces of Furniture

You can get a real buy on large pieces of furniture such as bureaus that are not of any particular period and are difficult to transport. If you're handy at repairs, paint finishes, etc., you can do very well.

Rugs

I've seen some wonderful Oriental, Persian, and Bukhara rugs that sell for a fraction of what you'd pay through a dealer. The better the condition of the rug, the higher the price will be, which is also true of size.

Patio Furniture Care

Your teenager greases up for a session of sunbathing. You left the cushions out and it rained during the night. Suddenly your beautiful outdoor furniture has stains and mildew spots all over the cushions. With proper care your outdoor metal, plastic, and redwood furniture should go on looking like new season, after season. Here are some tips from the folks at Brown Jordan, the manufacturers of all-weather outdoor furniture.

Wash Often

Use a mild solution of detergent and water. Rinse thoroughly and let dry.

Treat It Like a Car

Use automobile wax on the metal or plastic frame. It will protect it from the effects of sun exposure and salt air.

Removing Stains

For light stains use Soft Scrub. For heavy stains, use a product such as Comet. Scrub well, rinse, and use a vinyl protectant. Remove mildew with full-strength ammonia. As for fast-tanning products, they will stain your seats just as sure as your skin. Use Spic and Span or fabric cleaner full strength. And never use boiling water when spot washing. Warm is hot enough.

Personal
Spaces

Homestyle Trends

If you're curious about where you stand in relation to the rest of the country when it comes to your style of decorating, here's some interesting information. The Waverly fabric people sent a questionnaire to 1,200 individuals chosen at random from a list of some 7,000 consumers who had bought a copy of the Waverly *Idea Book of Decorating*. The response proved that people have a lot to say about their homes.

Traditional Style Number One

If your style of decorating is "traditional" you might not be surprised to know that you're in good company. Of those responding, over 78% said they are traditionalists and 73% saw themselves as practical.

Sophistication Quota

When it comes to avant-garde decorating, only 17% thought of themselves as trendsetters, but 44% thought of themselves as sophisticated.

Most Popular Trends

The most popular taste ran toward eclectic, a mixture of styles rather than one coordinated look.

English Country

Surprisingly, English country is more popular than American country. However, Colonial furniture is preferred over Victorian.

Contemporary

Only 4% said they preferred a contemporary style. It's nice to look at but hard to live with.

And a Word About Fabrics

Not surprisingly, florals were chosen by 86% as the favorite pattern, while checks and plaids were the least favorite.

Having the Blues

Almost everyone uses blue as the dominant color in a room, if not the entire house, and the least favorite color is black.

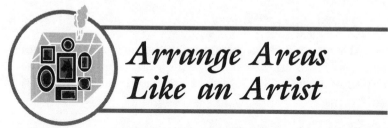

Arrange Areas Like an Artist

An artist looks at his or her home with a creative eye. Every corner of a room offers a chance to make an arrangement of colors, textures, and shapes that are pleasing to the eye. Look at your environment with an open mind.

Living with Color

When it comes to mixing bright colors, textures, styles, hard and soft crafts, the old and the new, there's no need to be timid. If you're an inveterate collector, create vignettes on all surfaces so that everything is arranged but seems uninhibited, as if it belongs there. If you like crafts, cover floors with colorful hooked rugs, drape patchwork quilts over sofas, and fill the walls with art and assemblages. If you do it well you can prove that more is definitely better!

Living with Folk Art

Combine early folk art with paintings, collages, and assemblages. If you have high ceilings, hang artwork as high as the eye can see. Suspend a colorful kite overhead. Create an arrangement of selected handcrafts such as a basket with two or three pieces of pottery on simple painted folk-art furniture. An eclectic mix of flea market furniture will add to the environment.

Living with Found Objects

Turn found objects into useful pieces of furniture. I've seen a lobster trap used as the base for a coffee table with a glass top cut to fit. Weathered driftwood can also become the base of a table.

Family Treasures

Select objects, awards, framed certificates, and photographs or prints of historic landmarks to create a wall of memorabilia around a fireplace or in a hallway.

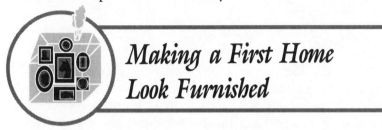

Making a First Home Look Furnished

You've just moved into your first home and don't have money to furnish it right now. There are many ways to make your home seem furnished so that it is comfortable for temporary living. Sheets are wonderful for creating a coordinated look throughout the house. They're affordable and pretty and they give you many decorating options. An unfurnished house echoes and sounds empty. By using lots of fabric you'll make your new home quieter and homier until you can buy soft furnishings, drapes, and carpets.

Curtains

Blue and white stripes, plaids, and checks create a wonderful country feeling. Use pinstriped single sheets for paneled curtains over sliders, French doors, or tall windows. Stitch evenly spaced ribbons along the top hem and tie to a painted dowel curtain rod. For shorter windows, cut a sheet to size for café curtains and tie to a rod in the same way. Use the same striped sheeting to make fabric bows across the top. A king-size sheet measuring 102 x 108 inches is equal to about 6 yards of 45-inch-wide fabric, which is perfect for a wide expanse of windows.

Dining Table

Use a metal outdoor table for dining in the kitchen or dining room and cover it with a blue and white plaid or checked sheet that drops to the floor. Place a lace cloth on top in the center. Fill a basket with pink or red geraniums for the center of the table.

Chairs

Buy the inexpensive molded-plastic outdoor chairs and make padded cushions for the seats and back covered with plaid sheets. Use striped sheets to make a ruffled flounce for the seat. It should hang down over the edge. Make square seat backs and ties out of the striped sheets for top and bottom cushions. The coordinated fabrics will distract from the outdoor furniture.

Floors

Scatter dhurries. They're inexpensive and light, especially for summer. Later, when you've invested in better rugs, you can use the dhurries in the bathroom or child's room. If you want to do some handcrafting, make a floor cloth with stencils and artist's canvas. Or, if the floors will be refinished or carpeted, consider painting them white and stenciling a design around the room. Or spatter paint the floor.

Bathroom

Use one sheet to make a shower curtain, then add a skirt around the sink with Velcro and a shirred sheet. Two pillowcases with borders make good-looking, temporary, no-sew curtains. Hang with clip-on curtain rings.

Bedroom

Stitch two corresponding sheets together to make a duvet cover for the bed. Mix and match pillowcases and shams to make the bed sumptuous. Buy one of those cheap round cardboard tables with a Lucite top for next to the bed. Cover it with a matching sheet that drops to the floor and fill the top with framed pictures, a vase of flowers, and other interesting, homey knickknacks.

Headboard

If you don't have a proper bed yet, do the following: Cut a piece of plywood to the width of your bed. Cover it with quilt batting, then a sheet to match the duvet. Bring the sheet edges to the back and staple in place. Set this lengthwise against the wall with a bed frame or just your box spring and mattress flush against it to hold it in place. For a little lift, make a frame from two-by-fours on end, then set the box spring and mattress on top. It will raise the bed enough off the floor for comfort and, combined with the headboard, will be quite good-looking. If the duvet cover doesn't go to the floor, you may need a bed skirt to hide the wood frame. Again, sheets to the rescue. Use an old plain sheet for the piece that goes under the mattress and make a skirt from a decorative sheet.

Occasional Furniture

Look for inexpensive wicker, outdoor folding tables, and folding bridge chairs that are adaptable. Cover the folding bridge chairs with slipcovers made from sheets. Most of the pattern companies have patterns for making bridge chair slipcovers.

Cover Worn Furniture

Use sheets to cover worn furniture that will eventually be replaced or reupholstered. Just tuck the sheeting in all around and tie it around the legs with a fat knot or bow. Wrap the cushions and pin to the underside. Stuff pillow shams with Poly-Fil and stitch opening closed for ruffled throw pillows.

Plant Distraction

Group lots of plants in corners that seem bare. For the kitchen counter, spray paint metal window boxes white and add a sponge treatment in a soft yellow. Fill with small pots of bright green herbs. Paper paint buckets are cheap and can be sponge painted as well to hold pots of plants.

Double Duty

A blanket chest can store blankets and linens and also double as a coffee table or end table. Stain an unfinished chest or paint it white. I prefer pickling or a milk-painted look for country style. Or pad the top and cover it with a sheet for a versatile ottoman/coffee table combination.

Finding Space for Home Work

A home office used to be the exclusive province of those who worked at home. But today, almost everyone needs an area reserved for "home work," whether it's for work we take home from the office, for filing and paying bills, or for working out of our homes. It's easier to be efficient in a well-planned work space.

How Big Is Big Enough?

A home office needn't be an entire room. It can be a well-defined corner of a room. A closet can be converted into a small work area for housing a desk, end to end, with built-in shelves and files on either side. A large dining room or kitchen often yields an out-of-the-way niche. So the first decisions are: 1. Where can you steal some space? and 2. Will you be comfortable working there?

Making Plans

Ask yourself the following questions:
1. What work will I do here?
2. How much space would I like?
3. How little space can I realistically live with?
4. What equipment do I need (i.e., typewriter, computer, adding machine, filing cabinet, etc.)?

What You'll Need

Make a list of everything you'll need on hand on the desk top and what you want hidden. Do you need shelves? How many? Drawers? Files? Stationery items? Storage for computer paper, reference materials, etc.?

Catalogs

Office equipment catalogs will give you ideas for setting up efficient work spaces of various sizes. They're fun to look through. A very complete mail order catalog with everything from portable computers to lighting systems comes out several times a year from Reliable HomeOffice. You can get a catalog by calling toll-free 1-800-869-6000.

Design an Office

Both Placewares (Boston) and Conran's (New York City) carry designer items in black and white (not the usual office colors) and the files, desks, bookshelves, and computer stands are intentionally small for home, rather than office, use. They are also better looking and cheaper than typical office furniture.

Specialties

Charrette's in Boston and Sam Flax in New York, both art stores, have catalogs of artist's drawing tables and architectural files, among other things. These can be functional for you even if this isn't your line of work. For example, you might be interested in an item called a boby (pronounced boh-bee). It's a compact plastic sectional taboret to hold art supplies and it rolls on casters. Everything fits neatly into the swing-out drawers and it's perfect in limited space. Great for a sewing room as well as a home office! This item is available at most art supply stores.

Make a Layout

Use graph paper to plan the layout. Draw each item to scale and in position. If you want to go further, you'll find room planning kits for around $30 at home centers. The one for kitchen designs has the right elements to use for designing an office. In fact, check out kitchen counters and cabinets if there's a showroom nearby. You can easily adapt these elements for your office space. Formica or Corian, traditionally used for kitchen countertops, are terrific surfaces for a desk. They're easy to clean, and if you use white or beige, the light reflects off it to brighten the work area.

Important Items

1. A comfortable typing chair is good for any office work. It rolls and fits neatly under a kneehole space.
2. Industrial carpeting muffles sound and is practical. It also defines the office area.
3. A good adjustable desk lamp is very helpful. The Tizia lamp with a halogen bulb is expensive, but is the latest in lighting technology.
4. Accessories: Don't adapt coffee mugs and drinking glasses for holding pencils. Try to find good-looking accessories that make your new home office look smart and businesslike.
5. A phone with a separate business line is a must.

Instant Home Office

It's easy to create an efficient desk for home office space. All it takes are two filing cabinets of the same height (but not necessarily the same style), a hollow-core door, three cans of spray paint (now available in decorator colors such as Aztec clay, English rose, and Wedgwood blue) and 8 yards of self-adhesive decorative shelf paper (marbleized or granite designs are quite attractive).

Files

Remove the drawers from the cabinets. If the files are rusty, sand them lightly. Using a back-and-forth motion, spray paint the entire surface of each file. Repeat on the front of the drawers.

Door

Cover the top and sides of the door with decorative paper, making sure the self-adhesive paper wraps to the underside. Smooth out all air bubbles with the palm of your hand or use a wooden yardstick. Turn it on edge and apply pressure while moving it from the center outward on each side.

Putting It All Together

Place the covered door on top of the file supports at each end. The trick to making this arrangement look good is the accessories you use. A great desk lamp is essential; a grouping of framed photographs, a pretty vase to hold fresh flowers, a small clock, and an interesting paperweight are a few suggestions.

Getting Ready for Guests

Having guests can be a welcome or dreaded experience. Because I live on a resort island, friends and family visit often. I find that a little planning can make the experience most enjoyable for all.

Plan Ahead

Part of this planning should include mapping out your own schedule, setting aside time to be with guests as well as time you'll each be pursuing your own activities. If you're working, plan time for purely sociable activities so you don't feel guilty when you do have to be away from your guests.

Everyday Things Aren't Ordinary for Guests

Doing routine things can often be entertaining for visitors. For example, I've found that taking guests with me to do errands is a great way to show them the island and what it's like to live here. Most visitors are surprised to find that not everyone is on vacation and enjoy seeing the behind-the-scenes life of those who live here. Your guests will enjoy knowing what your day consists of and getting to know your town in this way.

The Guest Room

No matter how small, a guest room can be comfortable and pretty. Here's a checklist.

1. If possible, the room should be devoid of any of your personal items in the closet and drawers.
2. A comfortable bed is extremely important. If the pillows are filled with feathers or down, be sure to have nonallergenic extras in the closet. It's nice to have plenty of pillows for sitting comfortably in bed to read, a comforter, and an extra blanket in the closet.
3. Keep the furnishings to a minimum. There should be a night table and reading lamps on each side of the bed, a small dresser, and a chair.
4. Accessories that make a difference include: a mirror (full-length is practical on the back of the door), a clock, a scatter rug on each side of the bed if the room isn't carpeted, and an outlet for a phone (the phone itself may not be necessary, just the availability for a private call). A small television is optional, and a fan may be needed.

Keeping Things Handy

A wicker trunk or blanket chest at the end of the bed is perfect for holding all the bed linens, and guests can put a suitcase on top.

Small Touches Mean a Lot

If it's summertime the following will make the room special: a linen table cover on the dresser with a vase of fresh flowers; light and airy curtains with a shade for privacy; lace-trimmed pillowcases; pretty pastel or pure white sheets freshly ironed; a basket of potpourri in the bathroom; and a basket filled with small bottles of shampoo, conditioner, moisturizer, and pretty soaps.

For Their Information

It's practical and considerate to leave reading material on the night table. It might include: the local newspaper, books about your area or books by a local author, a schedule of events, the information guide from the Chamber of Commerce, and a map of the area. If you know your guests' reading tastes you might take some books out of the library.

Extra Amenities

If your guests have special interests, check out local happenings before their arrival. For example, if they're interested in art or crafts you might find a show in the area. If you're having small children, look into events that might interest them. Plan for rainy-day activities and fill a basket with small toys to bring out when needed. If you have plans that don't include your guests, you might provide them with theater tickets for the night you'll be away from them, or leave the menus from several restaurants you think they'd enjoy.

Outdoor Living

If it's summertime, the patio, yard, or deck should be carefree and comfortable. Having guests is a good excuse to get your potted plants looking good. Set up a badminton or croquet set. A well-outfitted picnic basket is another nice touch to keep on hand.

Mealtimes

Plan meals ahead so that even you will feel like a guest. Make it easy for guests to help themselves or join in the cooking as an activity. Stock up on grocery items so that you aren't running to the store at the last minute. Change the everyday pace by using lovely table linens while your guests are with you. Use fresh flowers wherever possible.

Making Guests Feel at Home

When my daughters were little we went each year to visit my grandparents in Florida. What I remember best about those visits is that nothing seemed like a chore for them. Even when non-family members visited, my grandparents made them feel like part of the family, rather than an imposition. There may have been much preparation before we arrived, but while we were there everything seemed effortless. Planning your schedule, being flexible about it, letting guests help with whatever is being done, and feeling relaxed yourself will insure a good time for all.

Comfortable Bedrooms

I love to read, eat, watch television, and work from my bed. I once read that Sarah Bernhardt had an 8-foot bed that she traveled with all over the world, requiring special train cars to transport it and requiring that hotels remove doors and windows to install it in her suites. By comparison, my obsession with my bed doesn't sound so crazy. I never leave home with it.

It's relatively easy to create a private oasis within the

sometimes chaotic environment of a house filled with interaction and activity. When redoing your bedroom, think in terms of comfort, convenience, and visual calmness.

The Mattress

If you must replace a mattress, buy a good one. The extra expense will be worth it in the long run. (See pages 343–44 for tips on buying a mattress.)

Color

Choose a color scheme that's restful and promotes a feeling of calmness. If you like busy floral patterns, keep the colors soft.

Lighting

Lighting should be good for reading, i.e., the right height, brightness, and location. But also think about placing a small, dimly lit lamp in a strategic area to create another mood. Candles and soft music are a nice touch.

Windows

Plan window treatments for easy light control. Panels and a valance over sheers enable you to remove the heavier side curtains, leaving the sheers for summer. The valance stays put.

Comfort

A lightweight down comforter and pillows make a bed look so inviting. Use a pretty duvet cover over the comforter for easy care and bedmaking.

Pillows

Large, square pillows are great for sitting in bed and a small neck roll is pretty and practical.

Sheets

Sheets should be soft. Splurge and get good ones. Fancy, lace-edged sheets are a lot more expensive than plain white, but if you buy them unadorned, it's a cinch to add your own lace, eyelet, or ribbon to the top edge, at a fraction of the cost.

Carpets

Soft carpeting right at the spot where your feet first hit the floor is a must. If your floors are bare, place a small area rug beside the bed.

Night Table

The night table should be the right height for the lamp and for easy reach of your "stuff." Preferably, it should have a drawer or two and the surface should be large enough to hold essentials plus some pretty accessories, such as a framed picture and a vase of flowers.

Flowers

A vase filled with cut flowers, not a plant, is a great pick-me-up in the morning when you open your eyes. The flowers make the bedroom fresh and pretty even if it's a bit of a pain to keep replacing them. It's worth it.

Comfort from the Past

Something from the past is always comforting, like an old rocking chair, a quilt on the wall, an antique picture frame, or a vase.

Containers

Buy a large basket with a handle to hold magazines, books, hand cream, manicure items, tissues, pads, pens, etc., and keep it on the floor within easy reach. This will organize the things you don't want messing up your table, but it's easy to lift the whole kit and caboodle onto the bed.

Slip into Comfort

Can a family with children and a sense of style have a home that is comfortably chic? It takes a combination of oversized, "sink-into" furniture, slipcovers made from wonderful fabrics, and the absence of unnecessary accessories.

Ill-fitting Slipcovers

Slouchy, comfortable sofas and easy chairs covered with slipcovers that don't quite fit is a look that is especially appealing. The more the children jump on the furniture, the better it will look. Whether or not you have oversized furniture, slipcovers that seem slightly big, even fabric simply tucked in place, gives a room a certain quirky elegance. It's a departure from the perfect fit, which can be stiff and formal.

Fabrics Are Key to Success

The key to making this style work comes from the choice of fabrics used for the slipcovers. Textured, creamy white, linen-like, durable fabrics express a sense of quality. They are heavy but soft, the way they might be after many washings.

If White Is Too Radical

Floral patterned slipcovers often get better-looking with wear. When slightly faded, the furniture begins to look like family heirlooms. One conjures up an English drawing room with slipcovers in bold but faded floral prints, a roaring fire in the fireplace, books piled here and there, fresh flowers perhaps, but not much more on the tables than a cup of tea. Everyone feels comfortable in such a home. Those who can pull it off know that it requires the right window treatments and other accoutrements, such as good lamps, announcing that this is a stylish home as well as a comfortable one.

Dressing Down

Removing unnecessary clutter is essential. Less adornment leaves room for everyday clutter. A bare table is not necessarily stark. One great piece is better than a collection of mediocre items chosen just to fill space.

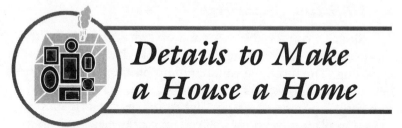

Details to Make a House a Home

A well-designed home is visually pleasing, but above all it's comfortable. Homes filled with family treasures, handmade crafts, personal collections, and an eclectic mix of furnishings are more interesting than those in which everything matches.

Flower Power

The natural beauty of flowers will enhance any room. The most appealing arrangements are those that are fresh and uncomplicated and look as though they've made the transition from country garden to tabletop with the greatest of ease. Flowers freshly picked from the backyard also serve to lift the spirits and often add a delicate scent to the room.

Soft Surroundings

Make any area of a room more inviting by adding a soft, luscious throw on a sofa, chair, or bed. It's surprising how such a small item can create ambience in a room.

Fabulous Folk

The renewed interest in hooked rugs and antique quilts, two items that are easy to use in decorating, makes it possible to add a special timelessness to a room. Folk art collections suggest an awareness of the value of things that have stood the test of time.

Art Appreciation

More people are discerning about art. They no longer buy a painting because it matches the color of a sofa, but because they like a particular artist's work. Buy what you like and can afford and you'll find a place for it.

Affordable Art

Look in old book stores and antique shops for early maps and watercolors of familiar places with special meaning to you. Then frame them in an interesting way.

A Gallery of Family Photos

Create a gallery for family photographs in an upstairs hallway. A unifying stencil design will enhance the arrangement.

Faux Chair Rail

Such a design might be a chair rail around the hallway where none exists. A stencil border is easy to adapt for this purpose.

Weave a Vine

For added interest, stencil a vine weaving around the rail. To do this use a leaf pattern and apply the design at random above and below the rail. Then, with an artist's brush, draw the vine to connect the leaves.

Arrange the Photographs

Arrange the selected photographs above the "railing." Consider starting at the top of the stairs with the earliest family photos and continuing in chronological order to the end of the hall.

Create a Home Sewing Center

Setting up an area for home sewing is easy if you have the latest and greatest tools and products. With the right equipment you can make an efficient area in the corner of a bedroom, inside a closet, or at a table in the family room. The following products will help.

Table Talk

The first item to consider is a 40 x 72-inch-long cutting table that shrinks to 18 x 40 inches for compact storage. It's called Cut-Above and is made by Smith Brothers (ask about this at home sewing centers). It's 35 inches tall, is made of a natural wood finish, and comes with a storage drawer and caster wheels. If this isn't in the budget, a hollow-core door or sheet of plywood on attached legs, saw horses, or file cabinets will give you ample cutting and sewing space. The file cabinets will provide the sturdiest support and you can use the drawers for storing fabric and other supplies.

Easy Sitting

A comfortable swivel office chair is good for sewing. This will enable you to adjust the height and will give proper back support. The swivel aspect allows you to swing from the sewing machine to ironing board with ease. It's also on rollers so you can slide it back and forth for ease in getting up and down between steps.

Lighting

A Luxo desk lamp with a mountable base is ideal for mounting on the side of a desk or to the wall. The swing arm gives you lighting exactly where needed.

Bulletin Board

Place a good-size bulletin board on the wall in front of the sewing machine or on a side wall. This will enable you to pin pattern pieces, fabric swatches, and notes within easy reach.

On the Wall

Place hooks on the wall to hold cutting and snipping scissors and other often-used items right where you need them, when you need them. No hunting around. Make a spool holder on the wall as well so that you can easily pick the color of thread you need for the project. A sewing area can be quite compact if you plan carefully so that every inch of space is used.

Storing Fabric

Shelves above the work surface will hold stacks of fabric within sight and will add to the visual interest of your sewing area if it's exposed. An inexpensive floor-to-ceiling storage unit of 9-inch squares and 13 inches deep (often sold through mail order catalogs from stores such as Crate 'N Barrel in Boston) is excellent for storing fabric and other supplies and doesn't take up much room.

Pinning It Down

Iris Pins are super fine and are perfect for holding patchwork pieces together.

Getting It Straight

An adjustable seam guide is essential. It's an attachment for your machine that enables you to make professional quilt blocks and perfectly straight seams every time. It pivots to three positions on a single slot.

Appliqué with Ease

Press-On Fleece is a product worth knowing about for making appliqués. It's made by Dritz and bonds to fabric for easy handling. It eliminates the step of basting or pinning fleece to fabric. If you're making gifts for the holidays, another product to know about is Woolly Nylon, a yarn-like thread that creates a very soft but strong edge or seam. It's ideal for serging napkins, tablecloths, and sweatshirts and comes in Christmas green and red.

Sewing Box

A well-stocked sewing box should hold different colored spools of thread, prewound bobbins, a good pair of scissors, pinking shears, pins, needles, a thimble, and a pincushion. This is a nice gift to give a home hobbyist. Add a few yards of pretty fabric and a pattern for making a pretty home accessory.

Instant Face-Lift

Give your house an instant face-lift for no money by rearranging the furniture. I am always moving furniture around in my house. Once I get used to an arrangement, I'm sure there's a better way to place the sofa, chairs, and tables. Shake things up a bit, if only for a while. In a month, you can put everything back again. If you're not sure how to do this, here are some suggestions.

Outdoor Furniture

If you have a rattan chair that you use outdoors, bring it in and put the overstuffed chair in another room. Add a pretty pillow to it and pull up a side table. Place a glass vase filled with cut flowers on the table and change them often.

Paintings

Change things around on the walls. Sometimes a change of wall treatment makes the whole room look a little different.

Angle a Table

Try angling your dining table. Add a large plant in one corner where the table's been offset.

Bed

Reverse the position of your bed and dresser for a change of scenery and a new perspective on the room.

Rugs

Remove the rugs for a while and consider bare floors or add scatter rugs, for an airy feeling.

Curtains

Use single sheets for curtains. Sewing isn't necessary as the edges are already finished. Attach evenly spaced ribbons across the top edge and tie to the curtain rod. Tie back with wide ribbons and make fat bows.

Paint

A change of paint color can do the trick and if you're not up for a complete room change, simply paint the window and door trims a fresh new color. For a quick pickup, add color to plain trims in the kitchen or an entryway. Paint the inside of a closet bright yellow!

Knickknacks

If you have lots of little knickknacks on tables and shelves, remove them and add one or two large items such as an oversized vase or a display of crocks.

Lamps

One way to change a look is to replace small table lamps with a standing room lamp. Halogen lamps equal the light of three small lamps and make a contemporary statement.

Shades

Add ribbon or tassel trims to window shades. Or use white doily shelf trim (it comes in a roll) and attach with double-faced tape for an instant and temporary shade trim. You can even add this to sheer curtains to give them a scalloped, lacy edge. When they need washing, simply peel the doily edge off.

Kitchens

Update Without Remodeling

According to many surveys by house remodeling experts, the kitchen is the room most often renovated. Since the kitchen gets the most use, we are quite demanding about how it should function. Perhaps the theory is that if the kitchen is state-of-the-art, the cooking will improve. However, if you can't rip out the appliances and cabinets and start from scratch, there are many things you can do to make a more functional kitchen. Some won't cost a cent.

The Cheapo Redo

If your kitchen is of recent vintage, reshuffling may be all you need to spruce it up. Systematically empty every single drawer and cabinet in the kitchen and get rid of everything you don't use. Then reline each drawer and shelf and reorganize everything in or on them. Think about how you use the kitchen (not always for cooking) and try to find a better location for all the stuff that's now spread about.

Color

White has always been the most popular color for kitchens, combined with wood cabinets. Repainting the walls and restaining the cabinets will give the kitchen an instant lift. For a splash of color add a wallpaper border, country-fresh blue and white plaid curtains, and a basket of red geraniums on the table. Add color with a plant or herbs on the windowsill. Keep a bowl of polished red or green apples on the counter.

Backsplash

A backsplash of floral tiles with an old-world English feeling adds elegance and charm. It's easy to install and an inexpensive way to update the look of a tired kitchen. If you can't afford to tile, a stencil design can be created to look like a border of tiles.

For Casual Entertaining

If you have the space, a center island with pull-up stools is a must. People are entertaining more casually and family life centers around the kitchen. If you can't afford to build it or don't have the space, you'll find freestanding islands on wheels that can be used wherever needed.

Make a Small Kitchen Look Bigger

Replace the cabinet doors with glass-front doors. Add porcelain knobs. Paint the walls and window trims white. Use a light wood or pickling stain on the cabinets.

A Little Goes a Long Way

Use Fleck Stone (a faux stone finish in a spray can) to change the look of old cabinets or countertops. It comes in different colors. Change all the knobs for more modern pulls. Add molding and decorative trim to the front of plain cabinet doors.

Open Shelves

If cabinets are old and inadequate, replace them with open shelves. They're more convenient, especially with children using the kitchen as well.

Sink Fixtures

Sink fixtures are changing all the time and this is a relatively inexpensive way to make your kitchen look more modern. There are lots to choose from and if this is the only change you're making you might feel you can splurge and get something you wouldn't buy if this expense were one of many.

New Fabric

If you have an eating area, make bright new seat cushions, placemats, and curtains. A fabric change can make it seem as if you've completely redone the room. Cover the floor with a rag or braided rug.

Getting Organized

If countertop space is what you need, clear away everything that's possible to put away. Find other convenient spaces for the small appliances that clutter the top of the counters. Look for small, wasted wall space where you can hang a set of shelves to hold everything in one area.

Floors

A new vinyl floor covering can add a subtle pattern to a muted neutral scheme. Black and white checks is a classic pattern for kitchen and hallway floors.

Looking Up

Lighting changes the look of a room. A new lighting fixture may make a big difference. It's easy to add fluorescent lighting under cabinets to illuminate countertops. Home centers sell them in different lengths and they just plug in.

Weeding Out

Get rid of dented pots, chipped plates, and that old coffee maker. If you update the things you use every day, your kitchen and you will be more spirited.

Quick Face-Lift for Old Cabinets

Remodeling a kitchen can be time-consuming, expensive, and inconvenient. However, there are some quick, inexpensive, and easy changes that can make a big difference.

Paint

Nothing makes a kitchen sparkle like newly painted cabinets. Spray-on enamels come in designer shades such as desert coral, English rose, hunter green, French vanilla, willow, Aztec clay, and Wedgwood blue. Plasti-Kote brand are water reducible and therefore ecological. They eliminate having to dispose of hazardous substances such as paint thinners and brush cleaners.

Stencil

Once you've repainted the cabinets, add a stencil border around the outside edge of each. You'll find a variety of precut stencil designs in hobby, art, and home center stores.

Fleck Stone

It only takes minutes to change the look of your cabinets with Plasti-Kote's spray-on faux granite. This product works on any surface. Create a quarry finish with any of the warm tones from the Southwest or the look of ironstone, marble, alabaster, or soapstone.

Color Wash

If your kitchen is dark, lighten and brighten it with a pastel color wash stain. Sand off the old finish, then rub the surface with a transparent veil of color such as peach, pale blue, white, or gray for a pickled effect. These finishes from Minwax stain and seal in one step. Easy soap-and-water cleanup.

Cracklin' Finish

From out of the past Plasti-Kote brings us the look of the future. It's the quickest, easiest way to spray on an antique crackled finish in the color of your choice and can be applied to wood, metal, or glass.

Sponging

One of the easiest faux finishes is sponging. Just clean the old surface and sand lightly. Mix an acrylic paint color of your choice and, using a natural sponge, dab the paint all over the cabinets. If the color is too light or dark when dry, apply a darker or lighter shade right over the first, leaving parts of the first color showing through.

Trim

For a custom look, add a simple wooden molding trim to the front of cabinet doors. Plain and decorative strips of moldings in all different sizes are standard items at hardware stores, lumberyards, and home centers everywhere. Finish with a coat of paint or a wood stain.

Knobs

Sometimes all it takes to give an old kitchen a face-lift is a change of knobs and pulls. Oversized white plastic door knobs are inexpensive and contemporary looking, as are the plain white, black, or red U-shaped handles. Decorative antique knobs or ornate drawer pulls can add character to an ordinary kitchen. Paint round wooden knobs in one color or with a checkerboard pattern. Add a flower decal or country symbol to the center of each painted knob. For a more casual look, paint each knob a different bright color.

Lining

Don't forget the inside of cabinets and drawers. It's always fun to find a colorful interior. Try a faux painted finish such as sponging on the inside. Create squiggly lines with two colors of paint. Elegant marbleized paper and pretty wallpaper make good linings. Con-Tact paper comes in a variety of contemporary designs and is easy to work with.

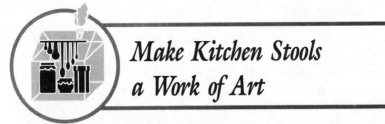

Make Kitchen Stools a Work of Art

Kitchen stools, bar stools, and utility stools are extremely useful. They can also brighten an area if you create a design on them. A variety of techniques are easy to apply. Start with the most common, unfinished wooden stools that are easiest to find in either 24- or 32-inch heights. Begin by sanding the wood smooth. If you are using previously painted or stained stools, remove the finish or at least sand so that you can repaint.

Pretty Paints

Paint the legs with one bright color and the round tops a contrasting color. Or paint each rung and leg different pastel colors. When using two colors, the darker shade should be used for the legs and the lighter shade for the top. It looks sturdier this way.

Savvy with Stain

Stain the legs with a dark wood stain and the top with a lighter stain. If you use an all-in-one product such as Wood-Sheen from Minwax, you can brush the stain and varnish on with one coat.

Check It Out

Paint the stools with semi-gloss white latex enamel. When it is dry, create a grid of tape over the entire stool top and, using a sponge brush, paint the exposed squares with blue latex or acrylic. When you remove the tape you'll have a blue and white checkerboard top.

Batik It!

Crayon batik is a wonderful technique that's fun to do, and the results look great. It's best used for creating a bright, colorful, childlike design. Begin by drawing a simple design on the stool top. This might be something playful from a child's coloring book. Using oil pastels or crayons, color in all areas of the design. Coat this with shellac, *not* varnish or polyurethane. When it is dry, add more crayon color for a brighter design, if desired, and shellac again.

Sponge Shapes

From an ordinary sponge, cut different shapes such as triangles, squares, and circles. Squirt a small amount of acrylic paint on a plate (it will wash off). Dab the sponge shape onto the paint and pat in a random pattern over the stool tops.

Marker Magic

Once the stool has been painted a background color, use a permanent marker to draw squiggly lines this way and that all over the stool top.

Decorate with Decals

Paint the entire stool and let it dry. Then cover the stool top with a collage of floral decals. To design your own, cut flowers from wrapping paper, greeting cards, or wallpaper. One giant sunflower makes a nice design in the center of a stool. Cut out leaves and vines to wrap around the legs. Add several coats of varnish or polyurethane to cover the paper.

Paper Patchwork

Choose a variety of patterned and colored wrapping papers and cut into squares and triangles to arrange in a crazy-quilt pattern on the stool. Or choose a traditional square quilt pattern to create with paper. Glue in position. The edges of the paper should wrap around the edges to the underside of the stool top for a finished look. Coat with polyurethane.

Padded Comfort

Once you've painted the legs, it's a cinch to upholster the seat. A large printed napkin, a calico print, or dishtoweling can be used to cover each stool. Cut the fabric so it is large enough to wrap around to the underside of the stool. Then cut a piece of quilt batting to fit the stool top and add some stuffing to the center. Place this on top of the stool and cover with the fabric. Pull the edges to the underside and staple all around.

Photo Montage

Create a montage of overlapping photographs or Valentine stickers and paste over the stool top. Use a decorative ribbon or upholstery tape to glue around the edge of the top to finish.

Dab It On

For the quickest and easiest finish, use a sponge-painting technique. Paint the entire stool with white latex enamel. Then choose another color for the sponging. Rip off a piece of natural sponge and dab it into the color. Using a light touch, apply it alternately with a rolling and tapping motion to fill in with color. Add a band of solid color around the stool's edge for a finishing touch.

Milking It for All It's Worth

An Early American milk-painted effect can be achieved by using fabric dye. Red or blue works best. Dilute the dye in a cup of boiling water. Use a sponge brush to coat the entire piece. It will soak into the wood and dry quickly if applied out of doors on a dry sunny day. Keep applying more dye to achieve a deep shade. Then dip fine sandpaper in soapy water and rub over the wood to create an unevenness of color with some of the natural wood showing through. This will make the wood satiny smooth. Apply a semi-gloss polyurethane over all.

Kitchen Collections

Look through your kitchen cabinets with a fresh eye. Almost any utilitarian objects can be used to create an interesting display.

Containers

If you have a variety of containers, jars, boxes, tins, or pitchers, arrange them all together on a shelf or countertop, along a windowsill, on top of a small table, or in a dry sink. They will look good and are practical for holding wooden spoons and cooking utensils within easy reach. Fill small pitchers with fresh herbs.

Baskets

Nothing beats the charm of baskets for their variety of shapes, sizes, and textures. Fill them with vegetables, fruit, and dry goods in canning jars. Keep everything natural for a harmonious grouping. An apple bucket filled to the brim is an open invitation for a healthy snack and looks great anywhere!

Bowls

White, oversized bowls, blue and white banded bowls, and yellow ware arranged on open shelves all make a bold country statement.

One Design Many Ways

It's fun to use one design in a variety of ways. After having her new kitchen painted Shaker blue, my Nantucket neighbor added a stenciled wallpaper border of a vine and doves above her kitchen wainscoting. She used the border paper to cut a stencil in order to repeat the design on her curtains and tiebacks. A dove hangs from a wreath on the door and echoes the stencil design throughout the kitchen.

Not Just for Beds

Quilts are not just reserved for bedcovers and wallhangings. Dress up the kitchen table for Sunday brunch with a patchwork quilted tablecloth.

Playful Centerpiece

Old wooden toys make a cheerful display in the center of the breakfast table. Create a setting or tea party with dollhouse furniture and dolls. Use early childhood blocks to spell out a greeting, such as "Cheers" or "Joy" or a birthday child's name.

Mix and Match

If you have a collection of mismatched plates, use them all together for an interesting table setting. I once found a pitcher at a yard sale. It's shaped like a chicken and the beak is the spout. Ever since, I've been collecting odd pitchers. Use any collectables to create a whimsical centerpiece. You'll be surprised at how creative you can be.

Kids' Korner

Decorating the Nursery

For many mothers-to-be, sewing for the nursery has become a popular activity during pregnancy. Not only is sewing cost-effective, but it can be a therapeutic exercise for relaxation during the nine months of anticipation.

When planning a baby's nursery, the Sewing Fashion Council suggests establishing a center of interest, usually the baby's crib. Begin your color scheme with a printed fabric, then repeat the colors on the walls, floor, and furniture.

Soft Furnishings

It's easy to make the soft furnishings such as comforter, curtains, cushion for a rocker, crib bumpers, and soft toys. Most pattern companies include these items.

Wallpaper

Walls can be the dominating element in the room. It's easy to hang wallpaper and there's a wide variety of patterns to choose from. But you can simply add a wallpaper border for an equally decorative look. Home centers carry a 6-inch-wide wallpaper border with a Beatrix Potter theme. Position it around the room a few inches above the crib. Then add a shelf above this for holding stuffed animals to match those in the design.

Instant Wall Decor

If you want to keep the work and cost at a minimum but still create designer impact, you might like to know about 3M brand Room Decorating Kits. There are twenty-two designs for a wall border that is backed with Post-it Notes adhesive. You simply stick up the 10- or 15-foot background border (it can be cut to any size) and then add the precut characters, moving the pieces around to design it yourself. It's as permanent or as temporary as you want. Since you don't have to paint or wallpaper, this is an easy way to decorate the walls.

Pretty and Practical

The following are some inexpensive, quick, and easy ideas for accessories to use in a baby's room.

1. Baskets for holding diapers, underware, lotions, etc. near at hand. Use for toys as well. A large basket with a handle is absolutely essential for quick pickups at the end of the day.

2. Ponytail ties for holding back curtains. They come with all sorts of cute decorations, fat buttons, and bows. Be careful not to use decorations that a child can detach and swallow.

3. Junior milk crates are small enough to line up on a dressing table or shelf to hold essentials.

4. Wall pegs for holding baby clothes, towel, sweaters, etc. give extra help to get the most-used items out of the way but still keep them within reach.

5. Memo pad above the changing table to jot notes, reminders of when baby was last fed, and notes for the baby-sitter.

6. Plastic stack bookcases are great for toys as well as clothes.

7. A space organizer sold for over the toilet can be used on a wall over the changing table.

8. Cut a regular mattress pad to the size of the dresser top and cover it with a terry towel or receiving blanket to use as a changing pad.

9. Inexpensive scatter rugs with rubber backing come with cute designs such as teddy bear or ducks. Use in front of the crib and dresser or rocking chair.

10. Stackable storage carts with open fronts are usually sold for kitchens but are great for holding baby's clothes.

11. Hang a large clock on the wall. It's decorative and practical.

12. For an inexpensive wall decoration buy colorful plastic picture frames to hold pages from a children's book. Make a grouping on the wall.

13. If you can't afford a rocking chair right away, buy one of the inexpensive plastic outdoor chairs and buy or make a padded cushion to fit inside the seat and back.

14. Another inexpensive idea for holding essentials over the changing table is a three-tier hanging vegetable basket.

15. Hang a net food umbrella (used to protect food at picnics) from the ceiling over the crib and attach a plastic toy or rattle at each corner for an inexpensive mobile.

16. A waiter's apron with two pockets is perfect to hang on the changing table or side of the crib to hold powder, lotion, etc.

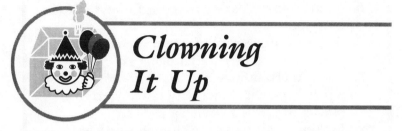

Clowning It Up

Clowns and balloons in bright primary colors make a happy theme for a toddler's room. Using fat, water-soluble markers (such as Faber-Castell's Posca Markers), it's easy to draw a clown from triangles and circles that can be placed on a variety of surfaces. Markers can also be used with stencil designs. Place a stencil cutout on your chosen surface and fill in the area with the colored marker. You won't have the messiness of paint and your child can help with the project.

How to Do It

1. Draw your own design, or trace a design from a coloring book. A cookie cutter can also be used to make an outline of a design.
2. If you use a coloring book design, after tracing it with a pencil, place the tracing face down on the chosen surface and rub the pencil over the back of the drawn lines on the paper to transfer the design.
4. Fill in all areas in the colors of your choice. Let dry.
5. It's easy to draw balloons with squiggly strings coming together and tied in a bow.

Wall Border

Create a border of tumbling clowns all around the room. Place a strip of masking tape on the wall to create a line above which you'll place the designs. Turn the clown design this way and that to create a row of clowns in different positions.

On the Furniture

Decorate the end panel of a crib or the front of dresser drawers with a row of clowns in various positions. My favorite is a trio of clowns holding balloons on the front of a toy chest.

Temporary Decorations

Water-soluble markers also work on glass and can be washed off. If you want a temporary window design, draw coloring book shapes on a window pane and when you tire of the design, wash it off.

Lamp Shade

Buy a plain, inexpensive lamp for a child's room, then use the small clowns to decorate the lamp shade.

Window Shade

Use the clown design to create a border along the bottom edge of a window shade. Add a large, colorful tassel for pulling the shade up and down.

Trash Can Transformation

You can transform any steel trash can into a whimsical storage bin for toys or a laundry container. All you'll need is self-adhesive paper, spray paint, and a pair of scissors. It's as easy as 1–2–3!

Decorate with Dinosaurs

Con-Tact makes self-adhesive border papers that come in delightful designs. There's a narrow border of colorful trains and another 6-inch-wide border sporting red, yellow, and green dinosaurs. Cut a piece of red adhesive paper to wrap around the trash can. Next, wrap a border of trains around the top and bottom rims, right over the red paper. Cut a length of the 6-inch dinosaur border to go around the middle of the trash can. Spray paint the lid with the color of your choice.

Make Your Own Designs

If you can't find the train and dinosaur designs, create your own by cutting out dinosaurs, trains, balls, balloons, etc, from solid-color paper. It's easy, and when you want to change the design, you simply peel away the adhesive paper and make another design or spray paint. The spray paint covers the galvanized steel beautifully.

Laundry Container

Use solid-color self-adhesive paper to cut out flower decals to decorate the trash can. Begin by spray painting the entire trash can in white. On the back of yellow paper draw a bunch of daisies with fat petals (no stems). Cut out each one. Use a quarter to trace green circles for the center of each flower. Cut them out and position on each of the flowers. Arrange the flowers at random all over the trash can and on the lid.

For Kids' Sake

There are many products designed specifically for kids. Some are meant to keep them safe and others to make their environments prettier.

Fire Prevention

The Home Safety Division of Funtech, Inc. introduced fire detectors that are easily mounted to the wall for practical use and pretty decoration. One, shaped like a Dalmatian pup, is called Petey-The-Puppy Firefighter, and the other is Big Red Firetruck. They come with a coloring book that teaches all about fire safety. For information write: Funtech, Inc., Home Safety Division, Dept. LL, 388 N. Ellicott Creek Rd., Buffalo, NY 14228.

Stick 'Em Up!

If you'd like to redecorate your child's room without much effort or expense, consider jumbo stick-ups. They can be applied to any wall surface, and it's a much easier and cheaper way to decorate than painting or papering. The designs can be affixed in a variety of ways and repositioned over and over again. Plus, the kids can do it themselves. Kits from Priss Prints include the Disney characters, Sesame Street, Barbie, Teenage Mutant Ninja Turtles, Berenstain Bears, GI Joe, My Little Pony, Batman, and Land Before Time. The 3M Company carries an extensive line of well-designed press-ons called the 3M brand Room Decorating Kit. My favorite of these is "Zoo Review." You'll find Priss Prints at home improvement centers as well as Sears and J. C. Penney. For the 3M products nearest you write to: Consumer Relations, 3M Room Decorating Kit, 3M Center, 515-3N-02, St. Paul, MN 55144.

Measure Up

One of the fondest memories a child has is being measured on the wall as a means of marking his or her height on a periodic basis. Unfortunately, these memories are gone forever when families move or redecorate. Priss Prints has a product called Growth Chart Kit. It's a mylar strip that measures to six feet and comes with frames to display photos of children alongside their measurements. The self-stick mylar film can be applied to painted walls, doors, and even wallpaper and can be removed and reapplied countless times without losing its adhesive or ruining the wall surface. The photo frames can also be lifted without harming the photos.

My Frame

When you see this product you'll say, "Why didn't I think of that!" It's a simple snap-together frame for children's artwork and is designed for horizontal or vertical wall mounting, or for tabletop display with the enclosed easel. The My Frame set includes six sheets of white drawing paper and makes the perfect lap easel for children to take while traveling. The frames come in pastel colors as well as red, green, yellow, and blue and are available in museum shops as well as home centers. For information and store locations call 1-800-331-9901.

Durable Furniture

Rubbermaid Specialty Products, Inc. includes super-durable children's furniture made of Resinite material. There are stackable chairs sized just right for children aged 4 to 7. You can stack them out of the way when you need extra space. The table has four pencil trays to make play and cleanup easy and they all come in blue, white, red, and slate. Rubbermaid's Space Organizer line includes clear, see-through stackable boxes of all different sizes. These make it easy to store clothes and toys.

Storing It All

And finally, speaking of getting organized, Closet Maid has the Kids' Kloset Organizer Kit, which allows you to expand your children's closet for maximum storage. The kit comes with three 24-inch shelves, one 36-inch shelf, two 41-inch support poles, and complete installation hardware. The Organizer Systems are made of heavy-gauge vinyl-coated steel construction and are durable and flexible. There are accessories such as the Kids' Kloset Stuffmobile, a three-drawer storage system; Stuffstacker; and Suddenshelf. Their booklet says that respacing is the art of getting twice as much stuff into the same amount of space. Call their national help line for any questions and a store location, 1-800-221-0641.

Children's Art

The illustrations from a children's book can be framed and arranged to create a delightful and inexpensive decoration in a child's room. It will keep a favorite story alive. Greeting cards are also good for this project.

Mounting

The pages can be mounted on a background of wrapping paper or wallpaper. Be sure the background print is dainty enough so it doesn't detract from the illustration. Cover the cardboard backing from a frame with the paper. Center the illustration carefully and glue in position. Rubber cement is perfect for mounting paper to paper, but you can also use white craft glue. Dilute it slightly with a little water so it isn't so thick.

Trim to Size

Some pages aren't the right size to fit standard frames, but they can be trimmed. Don't use scissors for this. To make a perfectly straight cut, use a metal ruler and a sharp razor blade. A plastic triangle (from an art supply store) will help if you plan to make an arrangement with several illustrations that require lots of trimming.

Fanciful Frames

You can often find small wooden frames at seconds shops and dime stores. It's easy to make a fanciful design by adding polka dots, squiggly lines, or dashes to the painted frame. Dip a cotton swab in acrylic paint and place dots or lines here and there. Your child might like to help with this.

Original Art

Mat and frame your child's original artwork. Some children's art looks amazingly like contemporary paintings and when framed is interesting enough to hang anywhere in your home.

Teen Decorating

The interest of teenagers is so volatile that any "room decorating" must be nonpermanent and versatile. While decorating might be out of the question, there are some things you can consider to make a teenager's room function better.

Walls

Wallpapering walls that will be covered with life-size posters seems a waste of time and money. So give the room a fresh coat of good paint that will withstand the taping and retaping of "removable art."

Furniture

Check the state of your child's mattress, especially if he or she has been using the same one for some time. A new mattress might be in order for the remaining years your child will be at home. A decent, adjustable office-type chair and desk are good investments that can be carried over for future use of the room.

Storage

Consider a compact unit made to hold books, records, and stereo equipment. When your child leaves home (eventually, they do), you'll be able to make good use of this if the room becomes a home office, guest bedroom, or den. Inspire your child to be neat by upgrading the room now.

Closet systems are designed to make the most of this space and pull-out wire baskets add easy-access drawer space for almost everything.

Self-Image

A full-length mirror in a teenager's bedroom and extra shelves for personal-care items could free up some bathroom time. Wall pegs encourage easy clothes hanging. It's not pretty to look at soiled shirts hanging on the wall, but it's better than seeing them lining the floor and pegs add extra space for these items.

Carpeting

Sturdy office carpeting is a practical solution for a teenager's room. If you carpet wall to wall, the room will look neat and trim and be easy to clean. Add some oversized floor cushions for seating. A duvet cover eliminates the need for a top sheet, and bed making is a cinch.

Small
Spaces

Living in One Room

While most of us don't live in one room, we are often faced with decorating small spaces. There's no need to feel cramped when you can make your home into a little jewel, chock-full of favorite collections. The following tips should help you live luxuriously in a small space.

Lightness Counts

Combine soft textures of white fabric on sofas and chairs with light wooden furniture to create restful, soothing space. Choose a monotone theme. If you must use color, choose soft pastels in much lighter tones than ever before. White with a drop of yellow or pink is preferable.

Clean and Neat

Clear away the unessential. This doesn't mean leaving tabletops bare. In fact, filling a tabletop with interesting items makes an important statement. The key is that every piece should count. Choose carefully what you display.

Large Is Better

This may surprise you. Hang large pictures close together, practically covering the walls. Small arrangements don't make as much of an impact.

Light and Sheer

Hang simple, sheer curtains made from fabric with a small, subtle pattern. Hang them from a single track on the ceiling and pull across the windows so they cover the entire wall, for one continuous look. For privacy, fit the windows with off-white, old-fashioned wood slat blinds. They're making a comeback.

Fool the Eye

Mirror the wall over the sofa. This expands the space visually. Mirrored wall sconces on each side of the windows is another visual trick.

Carpet

Use textured or subtle print carpets in pale earth tones. For a small space, wall-to-wall carpeting unifies the room and makes it appear larger. Consider an animal print carpet treated with Scotchgard for practicality.

Double Duty

Furniture pieces should do double duty. A tea table (usually 28 inches high) can be used as a coffee table in front of a sofa and will double as a dining table. Two side chairs can be pulled up to the opposite side and two more chairs can be used at each end if needed. Or use a round table of dining height as a side table and swing it around in front of the sofa when needed for dining.

Rich Accents

Oversized tapestry pillows add interest to a light sofa for winter. Change the covers to floral or plaid chintz for summer.

Sleep Area

An interesting daybed with a wood frame can double as a seating area and doesn't have to look like a bed in the living room. Cover with a fitted, textured fabric or crocheted coverlet and add an oversized bolster at the back. Pile with interesting pillows.

Make a Statement

One large interesting piece of furniture, such as an armoire, can house all clutter and will be a focal point in a room. A large piece in a small room must be practical and must look outstanding.

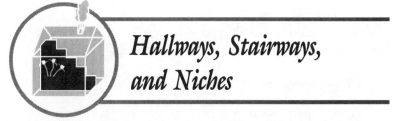

Hallways, Stairways, and Niches

Decorating a small area such as a hallway or stairway provides an interesting challenge. It's an opportunity to create a little vignette or display of paintings or collections in a confined space.

Country Charm

For a high-traffic area such as an entryway, consider a boldly painted or tiled checkerboard floor. One interesting blanket chest or chest of drawers in a milk-paint finish can hold an arrangement of country collectables. If there's a window in the room, place the furniture piece in front of this and top it with one interesting piece of folk art such as a whirligig. Add a Shaker-style row of pegs along one wall. Hang pretty straw hats.

Up the Stairs

A staircase wall is the perfect place for a collection of framed photographs or paintings of the same size. If you collect paintings of a particular subject, this is an interesting way to arrange them in one area of your home.

Cheaper Than Carpeting

Paint the top of each stair tread, then use this color with another to stencil a design on the risers. A wide border across each step will add interest to an otherwise plain area.

Alcove Allure

An alcove or niche in a room can be designed with the eye of the artist arranging a still-life painting. Take ordinary objects that you use daily and creatively arrange them as if you were setting the scene for a photograph.

Overpower with Flowers

A tiny space, such as a niche under the stairs or a dead corner or an entryway too small for furniture, is perfect for pots of flowers. Clay pots filled with pink geraniums will evoke the romance of summer. Use lots and lots of them bunched together and in pots of all different sizes. Arrange them on the floor and at different levels. In this case more is definitely better.

Attic Bedroom

If you have a small attic room, plan a delightful area for a writing desk under a sloping roof. Use limited wall space for an arrangement of small antique framed photographs or watercolors. Grouping them tightly is more interesting than spreading them apart. Find unusual desk accessories at flea markets or yard sales or use interesting containers to hold pens, letters, etc. Keep a small vase filled with fresh flowers.

Cottage Makeover

Creating an interesting environment in a small space can be challenging. First determine how the space will be used, then carefully choose each element for looks as well as dual function.

Color Is Key

A coat of white paint makes everything fresh and clean and makes a small room seem bigger. A subtly sponged faux finish will add interest with texture. This is a good wall treatment for small areas such as a bathroom or hallway. A nice accent color is plant green, which creates a fresh outdoor feeling. Use hanging plants for decorative touches.

Theme

Use one predominant fabric print and color throughout to unify the space.

Window Treatment

No heavy drapes. Use minimal curtains over small windows. Bottom cafés with a top valance in sheer fabric will lend privacy and let the light in. A stenciled ivy design around the window frame will visually enlarge the windows and connect the outdoors with the inside.

Keep Furniture Light and Low

Light and scaled-down furniture such as wicker is comfortable and summery. The seat cushions can be covered in your choice of fabrics. Accent with small throw pillows in a contrasting fabric of the same color scheme.

Ready-to-finish wooden furniture is perfect for pickling with a white stain or painting with a glossy white. Choose small tables and use one large piece, such as an armoire, to store the television, VCR, stereo, and other equipment. If you keep all the furniture at a low level, one tall piece can add interest if it's light in color. A dark, large piece will overpower the room.

Storage Solutions

Use a series of unfinished low cabinets or dressers along one wall to create storage with a built-in look. Finish with a semi-gloss paint or light stain. The top can be used as a buffet, to hold collectables, lamps, books, etc.

Plan the closets to take advantage of space-saving conveniences. A blanket chest provides ample storage for bulky sweaters, linens, and off-season clothes. It can also serve as a coffee or side table.

Kitchen

There are many small appliances on the market that function well and look good. Replace kitchen cabinets with open shelves. Everyday items become another decorating element.

Floor Covering

Sisal carpeting is a light and practical floor covering. Paint the floor a light color. Pickling is a light treatment for wood floors.

Built-in Bed

If you're handy and enjoy small building projects, a built-in cupboard bed, Swedish-style, is a good solution for a narrow bedroom. Shelves at the end of the bed hold books, even a small television. Drawers underneath eliminate the need for bureaus, and the custom-built wood frame can be painted, stained, or covered with wallpaper or fabric.

Bedroom Dressing

Pay attention to the bed. It is the largest element in the room. Pure white, lace-edged linens and a down comforter will make any bed look inviting without overwhelming the room. If the room is especially small, use soft colors such as peach or rose to create a cozy nest. For a dramatic treatment, wallpaper the walls and ceiling and cover the bed with fabrics to match. Don't use a large print.

Dormer Drama

Many houses have dormers and they come in all shapes and sizes. Some are just one window width, others are shed dormers that go across the entire roof expanse. Many consist of a double window and measure out at 6 to 8 feet wide. Others are just a small window width. They provide light and head room where the slant of the roof limits the standing space inside. How are these dormer spaces used?

Dormer Dressing

If you have a dormer in the bedroom, use the space for a dressing table. Yard sales, thrift shops, and discount stores are good sources for dressing tables. Or cut a shelf to the desired depth and width to fit between the dormer walls. Then add a fabric skirt to the front. Use a pretty sheet to make the skirt and attach with Velcro.

Add Personality

Use the same sheet pattern to make a window treatment and a gathered skirt for a stool or for a pillow on a small straight-backed chair. The walls can be covered with wallpaper or fabric, or give them a paint treatment. Since this is a small area, you can have fun with color and faux finishing if desired.

Finishing Touches

Attach a lamp on each side of the wall and place a small tabletop mirror on the shelf or dressing table. Find a pretty tray or baskets to hold cosmetics to complete the scene.

Dormer Desk Niche

This recessed area is perfect for a home office. Have a length of wood cut to fit between the dormer walls or use a hollow-core door cut to size. Support each end with a file cabinet or small dressers with drawers. Add shelves on the dormer side walls if needed.

Simple Window Treatment

Miniblinds are perfect here. Soften the look with a padded fabric valance at the top. It's easy to make a wooden valance, then pad with quilt batting and cover with an appropriate fabric, which is stapled in place.

Dormer Seating

A dormer is perfect for a window seat. Plan to have a platform cut to size, then add a fabric-covered foam cushion and some pretty pillows at each end. Wicker baskets or a trunk can be used underneath for storage. Or, if you're handy, add doors to hide clutter under the window seat.

Sitting Pretty

For seating without building, a loveseat can be easily set into a dormer niche with a small coffee table in front. This creates a cozy reading area or a place to have an informal meal. If it's in the bedroom, this can become an area for quiet respite away from the main living area of the house. Café curtains or delicate lace panels are perfect for the windows, but heavy drapes will overwhelm the area.

Space for Storage

If the dormer is in a child's room, plan to use this space for storage. Build shelving at windowsill level on all three sides of this "room," and use the top shelf of all the units to display stuffed animals, a dollhouse, etc. Con-Tact has a self-adhesive paper that sports glow-in-the-dark stars, which might be fun for the ceiling where the roof slants. Or wallpaper this area with whimsical paper to make it special.

Special Treatment

Whatever use you choose for your dormer, treat it like a separate room, even though it's small. The limitation of size will be an advantage when planning its use and decoration. It might become a cozy cocoon, completely enveloped in pretty wallpaper and soft furnishings, or it can be contemporary and sleek.

Fabric
Finesse

15-Minute Makeovers with Sheets

Sheets and pillowcases are terrific for use in making inexpensive, instant changes. Use them temporarily to cover upholstered furniture for the summer. Just drape and tuck here and there for a loose, casual fit. Sheets feel wonderfully cool to the skin and are easy to wash. Many of the sheet companies come out with pretty springtime patterns early in the season and some have ruffled edges or eyelet hems.

Cushion Covers

Use large pillow shams to cover seat cushions. Just slip the cushion inside and tuck the excess fabric under the back of the seat.

Sofa Cover

Use a large flat sheet to cover sofa cushions and secure underneath with safety pins to anchor and keep the fabric from coming loose when someone's sitting on it.

Table Cover

Use a double bed sheet to drape over a dining table. The edges are already finished; no sewing of hems is required.

Sideboard Cover

A sheet with a ruffled or pretty trim on the top edge is perfect for a sideboard. The untrimmed side is placed to the back and the sides won't matter. Or add iron-on seam binding in a contrasting color all around. No sewing needed!

Instant Curtains

Use single sheets with a pretty border for curtain panels. Attach ribbons with straight pins (or iron-on seam binding) evenly spaced along the top edge and tie to the curtain rod.

Colors That Look Best

For a coordinated look, combine prints and matching solids. Dark pastels look like better fabric than light pastels. Use decorator colors and the fabric won't look so much like a sheet. For example, use forest green rather than aqua, raspberry rather than pale pink.

Use Sheets Unwashed

Don't wash the sheets before using them. Inexpensive sheets are really the best because they are slightly stiff and therefore more crisp looking. They will be limper and softer after washing, which is great for the bed but not for decorating.

No Sewing for Cut Edges

If you have to cut a piece of fabric to cover a small end table, for example, tie a fat knot at each corner to finish the edges in an interesting way. Again, no sewing required.

Cool Bedroom

Use a large, floral-print top sheet as a bedspread to keep the bedroom looking cool and summertime fresh. Pick out the solid colors in the sheet to cover the night tables. Cut the ruffle off the top of a sheet and tape (double face) to the edge of the window shades for temporary decoration.

Pillowcase Covers

Pillowcases are terrific for covering the plastic, padded seats on wire chairs. Look for pillowcases with a decorative border. Just slip the case over the seat pad and stitch across the open edge.

Outdoor Cushions

A single sheet can be used to make four oversized 20- to 24-inch pillows for a bench in the garden or on a deck. For each pillow cut two pieces of sheeting 2½ inches larger than the pillow form all around. With right sides facing, pin the front and back together and stitch around three sides and four corners, leaving one edge open. Turn right side out and insert pillow form or fill with stuffing. Gather the excess fabric at each corner and tie a ribbon around the fabric. Each corner will look as if it has little bunny ears. When the cover needs washing, just untie the corner ribbons and slip it off.

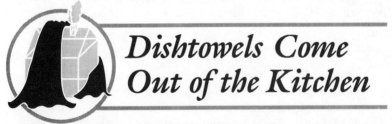

Dishtowels Come Out of the Kitchen

Dishtowels and linen dishtowel fabric, sold by the yard, are ideal for a variety of decorating treatments.

Napkins

Dishtowels make the best inexpensive cloth napkins and they're practical as well. I'm always on the lookout for linen dishtowels that are on sale. When cut in half you have two napkins for a fraction of what you'd pay for cloth napkins. Turn the raw edge under and stitch for a quick and easy project.

Terry cloth dishtowel napkins are perfect for backyard barbecues when you want something stronger than paper. After dinner, simply toss them in the washing machine. No ironing necessary.

Patchwork Tablecloth

Did you know that you can buy dishtoweling by the yard in red, green, or blue and white plaid? Sold in most fabric stores, it is 18 inches wide and is wonderful for making an easy patchwork tablecloth. Simply cut two different colors into 9-inch squares (you'll get eight squares per yard), arrange them in a patchwork pattern by alternating the colored squares, and stitch together. It makes a pretty and practical country cover.

Café Curtains

Use linen dishtowels to make café curtains with a valance. (See pages 40–41 for no-sew cafés.)

Pillows

Country throw pillows are easy to make. Stitch two blue and white plaid dishtowels together, leaving a small opening on one side. Turn inside out, stuff with Poly-Fil, and stitch closed. Make smaller pillows by cutting squares to the desired size from a large dishtowel and combine them with the larger pillows on a bed or sofa. You'll have an instant country look.

Chair Seats

Use dishtowels to cover foam rubber seat cushions and add matching chair back cushions with ribbon ties. And here's another idea: Use the shape of an animal as a pattern for your kitchen chair backs. To do this, cut the front and back pieces, shaped like a pig, for example, from dishtowels. Cut a piece of thin quilt batting slightly smaller for the padding and stitch together as you would for a pillow. Add a button eye if desired.

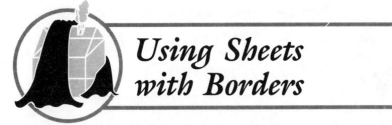

Using Sheets with Borders

Just as I was poring over Burpee's spring catalog and actually believing I could create a garden exactly as pictured, a catalog arrived for a new line of sheets. Just in time to save me from disappointment! Since I have never actually produced a garden of any significance, it seems that thinking of creative ways to decorate with flowered sheets rather than flower seeds is more realistically suited to my particular talents.

Shower Curtain from a Single Sheet

A single bed sheet is perfect for making a shower curtain. Choose a sheet with a wide corresponding border to use at the top. You'll find a complete packet of grommets and the grommet tool in hardware or home centers and in some five-and-ten stores. It's easy to attach them, evenly spaced across the top edge of the sheet. Add a plastic liner when hanging.

Dressing Table Skirt

A sheet with a pretty border is also perfect for making a dressing table skirt. Choose a sheet with a border pattern that can be used across the bottom hemline.

Prints for the Garden

Large florals are quite pretty on garden furniture. Cover pillows and cushions in colors to match the flowers in your garden. One single sheet goes a long way. Use the border to make a pillow ruffle.

Carefree Creative Coverings

If you dislike your living room sofa but can't afford to buy a new one, a slipcover might be the answer. Slipcovers infuse fresh color and style to a sofa or chair. Trims, cording, and tassels make good accents.

Easy to Make

Slipcovers are easier to make and fit with the help of ready-made gathering and pleating tapes. Different styles work best with different fabrics. For example, a floral garden print looks better with gentle shirring than with a strictly tailored style. Wider widths of fabric such as 90- and 120-inch fabric make coverings easy because there is less piecing. Fabric stores carry these wider fabrics in their home decorating sections.

Tips from the American Home Sewing and Craft Association

1. Color is the single most important element in a room. Color can make a room seem larger or smaller, lively or calm, warm or cool, open or cozy,

casual or formal. Choose colors to fit your life-style.

2. Select one color as the dominant hue and accent with coordinating or contrasting colors. Bold white accents add flashes of light to a dark room.

3. Look for fabrics that have stain-resistant seals.

4. When figuring yardages, consider hems and seam allowances.

5. Accurate measuring is key to the success of any home sewing project.

6. Start with a good metal tape measure.

7. Measure height, width, and depth where necessary.

8. Make a small line drawing of the object to record measurements of each section.

9. The gathering ratio for shirred pieces such as a dust ruffle is usually 3 to 1.

10. Special sewing machine feet can make sewing quicker and easier. Try using a roller foot, narrow hem foot, ruffling foot, and piping foot.

Patterns

There are many patterns for easy slipcovers put out by such companies as Vogue, Butterick, and Simplicity.

No-Sew Solution

If you want a quick, no-sew solution, simply drape a queen- or king-size sheet (depending on the size of your furniture) over the sofa or chair and tuck it in wherever possible. Gather the fabric around the legs and pin in the back. Wrap each of the cushions and secure underneath. This slouchy chic look is popular with families that include small children. No need to worry about sticky fingers. When it's dirty, just toss in the wash. Best of all, the fabric is wide enough for no seaming and is relatively inexpensive as far as slipcovers are concerned. There is a wide range of patterns to choose from.

No-Sew, Foolproof, 5-Minute Designer Slipcovers

Recycle an outdated or outgrown skirt, such as one with a flower print from Ralph Lauren that has a wonderful, summery feeling. With the zipper to one side, slip the skirt over a seat cushion, adjust the fabric so it's smooth and taut, and tuck the excess under the seat. Pin if desired, but it isn't necessary. Great on a wicker chair!

French Country Style

While traveling through the south of France, I was taken with the fabrics of Provence. The colorful printed cottons are used for tablecloths in restaurants, curtains in country homes, for scarves and tote bags. The variety of inexpensive prints has a country charm that is reminiscent of traditional calico used in early American designs. They are imported here and sold through specialty stores such as Pierre Deux in New York City. Waverly fabrics has a similar line that can be found in most better fabric shops throughout the country.

Table Covers, Quilts, and Chair Seats

As with calico, it is easy to combine patterns and colors and still have a coordinated look. Some of the prints are banded with a contrasting border of a larger design. Use these for making tablecloths, napkins, and quilts. Consider too making quilted chair seat cushions and secure them to the chair backs with fabric ties.

Pretty Details for Curtains

Decorative tiebacks add a custom look to curtains. This is an easy project to make with one yard of any fabric. Ideally they should be approximately 4–5 inches wide. Cut a strip 36 inches long, allowing ¼ inch for seam allowance at each end with a little over 17 inches at front and back of the curtain. The suggested width of 4–5 inches is perfect for long panels. If you use a fabric with a decorative border, the width of the fabric will be determined by the design. When possible, use the full print rather than cutting away part of it to make a narrower tieback. I often use a fabric liner to give the tieback a little body.

Valances

The borders alone can be used to make a valance over café curtains in a kitchen or dining room. In most French country towns, the windows are covered with lace panels. These provide privacy and allow light to fill the room. A pretty bedroom treatment is a combination of lace panels with a padded wood valance covered with provincial fabric. Or simply use the fabric to make a gathered valance over lace curtains.

Lace by the Yard

When I first visited Paris many years ago, I thought these curtains had all been hand crocheted. Perhaps at one time they were, and indeed, during this trip, I saw women in the town square of Bram, a tiny village in the south of France, crocheting lace curtains. But for the most part, the lace is purchased by the yard just as other fabrics are sold. Fabric shops here, as in France, sell a wide variety of patterns. Ready-to-hang lace panels in a variety of window sizes can be found in most fabric shops.

Formally Speaking

For a formal country window treatment, cover a window with a lace panel and then add printed cotton draperies. The lace panels should hang flat to show the patterns. Use simple wooden or brass rings for hanging the draperies. Add wide tiebacks and you will have a charming French country feeling.

Charming Bath Ensemble

For instant freshness in the bathroom, make a lace café curtain. It should be quite full. You'll need 2½ times the width of your window and the hem should be full as well, about 3 inches. Use a piece of the printed fabric to trim towels and for lining a basket to hold soaps. This is an easy and inexpensive way to add a bit of French country style to your home.

Industrial Materials for the Home

Good, sturdy, industrial-type materials have always attracted interior designers. They're inexpensive and great-looking.

Ticking

Mattress ticking is a practical fabric that has multiple uses. It's always in style for upholstery, as slipcovers, and for use as curtains and shades. Recently I used it for Roman shades that are easy to make. When pulled up, the folds create a striped valance effect. Ticking material is inexpensive. If you wash the fabric and use it wrong side out, it will be softer in both feel and appearance. The navy blue looks like gray, which is sometimes preferable.

Muslin

Muslin is another of my favorite fabrics. Unbleached muslin is ecru or a yellowy beige. Bleached muslin is a soft white. When washed and unironed it is slightly crinkled and is wonderful for quilt projects. Substitute this for any white fabric and your project, whether a quilt or curtains, will have character. A big bonus with muslin is that it's not only inexpensive (sometimes as low as $2 or $3 a yard), but it can be found on bolts from 36 up to 90 inches wide.

One of its characteristics is that natural light filters through it while it lends privacy over windows. If you use a down comforter on your bed, this material is perfect for a light duvet cover. Stretch it over artist's canvas to use as a room divider or folding screen.

Parachute Nylon

Parachute material is sold by the yard, just like other fabrics. It is often used by photographers to filter light or as a backdrop for portrait photos. This material is wide and billowy. It's excellent for tall windows. Bring it up one side of the window and swag it over a curtain pole at the top so the material drapes in a graceful curve, hooks over the pole, and hangs down behind it. No cutting, hemming, or sewing needed; it's totally carefree. For privacy add paper accordion shades. It's an all-white treatment that is soft, crisp, and easy.

Brown Paper

Kraft paper, used for wrapping packages, can be used as wallcovering. The neutral color goes with everything. It's smart-looking, inexpensive, heavy-duty, and easy to use. It can be applied with rubber cement or wallpaper paste. Once it is in place and dry, you can coat it with glossy polyurethane for a slick finish. Be sure to read all labels so that your adhesive and finish are compatible.

Drop Cloths

Painters' drop cloths are made of heavy, inexpensive fabric. They are most commonly found in natural colors but also come in rose, gray, and pale blue. Use them for canvas slipcovers on folding bridge chairs, cushions, and pillows. Add decorative braids and trims for color. Spatter paint a drop cloth for an interesting table cover.

Where to Find It

Ticking and muslin (sometimes called ecology cloth) can be found wherever fabric is sold. Parachute fabric is sometimes offered through photographic catalogs. Drop cloths are found in paint and hardware stores and home centers. Other industrial materials are found in mail order catalogs. Be creative when looking through catalogs. Materials meant for offices can be adapted for home use with surprisingly good-looking results.

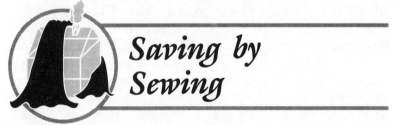

Saving by Sewing

Take stock of areas in the house that could benefit from a new fabric replacement. Sewing is a relaxing and fulfilling way to spend a weekend at home, and making your own home accessories can be quite cost-efficient. The new sewing machines do everything but cook a meal. If you need a push to get started, there are lots of easy weekend projects that take an hour or two to complete.

Home Decorating Patterns

Most of the pattern companies have added a home fashion section to their pattern books and you'll find designer shades, balloon curtains, and fancy drapes, as well as patterns for tablecloths, chair cushions, seat backs, slipcovers to dress up folding metal bridge chairs, and even fanciful tea cozies.

Patchwork Duvet

You can make a duvet cover for your comforter in less than an hour by stitching two pretty sheets together. Or make an interesting patchwork duvet by stitching together enough 5–6-inch squares in alternating colors to create the overall size needed. Use a solid sheet in the appropriate size for the back and leave the top edge open to insert your comforter. Attach Velcro, buttons, or snaps evenly spaced across the top for closing.

Pot Holders Are Practical

How often do you replace your pot holders? It's so easy to whip up new ones in bright colors or even shapes. An Amish quilt pattern in a typical color combination of black, purple, deep red, and dark green is terrific-looking.

Cover Exposed Pipes

If you have an old-fashioned sink with exposed pipes below, make a fabric skirt to attach to the sink. Velcro is the best way to attach the gathered fabric to the edge of the sink.

Napkins from Leftovers

Pretty napkins are easy to whip up from a bunch of remnants. Buy a little bit of every fabric print that attracts you. From a half yard of fabric, you'll get two generous napkins of 18 inches square. With the cost of cloth napkins skyrocketing, hemming four edges of fabric is a cinch.

Wallhanging

A quilted wallhanging is an interesting and inexpensive substitute for a painting. Use pretty remnants of fabric. Fabric shops often sell quarter-yard rolls cut especially for quiltmaking. Make your project 45 inches square, which is exactly the width of most fabrics, and you will only need a total of 1½ yards for the top and 1½ yards for the backing (this can be muslin). You'll find a variety of patterns in any quilt book.

Always a Place for Placemats

If you're crazy about the more expensive fabrics, you won't need much to make a set of elegant placemats. Try floral chintz. Use a plain fabric backing and save the good stuff for the top. Make them slightly larger than the ones you buy and add interest with a second stitch line in a contrasting thread color half an inch in from the edge all around.

Small Comfort

A crib quilt in a simple patchwork or appliqué pattern is easy, practical, and fun to make. Choose a pattern that is a repeat of one shape, such as a rectangle. In this way you can cut all the pieces at once and there are no complicated directions. The excitement comes from the choice of fabric and the arrangement of the fabric pieces. I like to use soft pastels on a baby's quilt. The colors and the fabric get softer and look better with each washing. The quilt lined with thin cotton batting is a good lightweight covering for the summer. Use traditional batting for a warmer cover.

Seamless Seems Easier

Some of the fabric companies sell 90-inch-wide fabric to eliminate seams in home sewing. Springmaid, for one, has a line of cotton chintz prints at affordable prices. McCall's has patterns for a canopy, fabric screen, shower curtain, and drapes that use the 90-inch-wide fabric. This is a real contribution for quiltmakers as it is now possible to back a quilt with fabric that doesn't require seaming.

Craft Explosion

Fabric shops now carry craft supplies because the pattern companies are including craft projects in their pattern books. Bandbox patterns that require no sewing can be found in the Vogue and Butterick books. Vogue has introduced a lavishly embroidered pillow pattern trimmed with braid, tassels, and ribbon. Elaborate window treatments are contained in Butterick's Windows in a Weekend package.

Take One Pillowcase

Turn a pillowcase into a pretty laundry bag or garment cover you can make in minutes. All you need is a pillowcase, a hanger, and 5 feet of drawstring cord or clothesline.

Laundry Bag

Stitch a ½-inch channel around the inside edge of a pillowcase hem. From the outside, make a slit in one side seamline of the channel. Attach a safety pin or paper clip to one end of the drawstring cord and weave through the channel. Pull to gather. Knot each end and tie for hanging on a closet hook.

Garment Bag

Turn a pillowcase inside out. With the open edge at the bottom, center the hanger on top of the other end of the pillowcase with the hook end above the fabric as it will be when hanging. Fold each corner edge of the fabric down over the hanger to conform to its shape. Remove the hanger and press the fabric. Open the edges and stitch along the pressed lines. Cut away excess material ¼ inch above the stitch line.

Find the center of the top edge of the pillowcase (not the open end) and make a ½-inch slit across to insert the hanger. Fold the raw edges of the slit to the inside and press. Stitch across each folded edge. Turn the pillowcase right side out and press. Slip hanger inside and pull the hook through the opening.

Wake Up
with Color

Color
Sense

Color can solve decorating problems, create a certain mood, and evoke different feelings. Inspiration for color schemes often comes from nature. Fruits and flowers contribute greatly to color choices for fabrics and paint.

White

White opens spaces and highlights architectural details. If you're creating a room around a white scheme, introduce natural colors in textured items such as a sisal rug, an old piece of furniture that has been partially stripped of white paint to reveal the wood beneath, a creamy damask fabric, and ceramic accessories. Fill an old laundry basket with dried flowers. Use animal prints in browns for throw pillows on a white canvas sofa. Add terra-cotta pots for plants and an arrangement of pottery on a wood or linen-covered table.

Blues and Greens

These colors will make everything watery and cool. Combine accents of aquamarine, cobalt blue, lilac, even floor stains in pale blue. These colors work well where the room gets lots of sun and you want a cooling effect. It's a very summery scheme.

In the Pink

Pinks are easy to live with. They are good in daylight and at night. This is a popular color, in any shade, for bathrooms. Shades of pink add a rosy glow to the bedroom. Try summer slipcovers in rose chintz with pink and white ticking. Use a touch of lavender for accents. A pink glaze is nice on entryway walls.

Sunny Yellow

Use this color for instant sunshine. It's a lively color for dishes, lamp bases, wicker in a sunroom, for bathroom wallpaper. Use a yellow floral print fabric for wicker cushions with yellow and white checked pillows. Pin-striped yellow and white curtains are nice anywhere. A yellow urn filled with yellow roses is offset by the bright green leaves. Sponge paint yellow on clay pots to hold orange hibiscus.

Peachy Glow

Peach is always warm. Add mint green for accents as well as deep green and a touch of yellow. This is a nice combination for a dark room that needs an uplift.

Green

Deep green chinaware on a dark table with the palest yellow walls is sensational for a dining room. Use a deep red floral fabric—lots of it.

Teal Blue and Yellow

This will create a soft but exciting combination. Accent window trims with grayish blue paint. Stripes in muted colors for wallpaper or fabric are always classic.

Blue and White

This combination says "summer." Paint the floors white, add wicker or willow furniture, and cover cushions and tables with blue and white plaid, checks, stripes. Accent with touches of yellow sunflowers, a needlepoint pillow, and dishes. Pin-striped blue and white curtains are fresh and simple. Tie to a painted dowel with bows made of the same fabric.

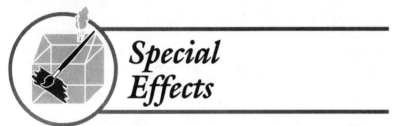

Special Effects

Buy a can of paint. It's the best way to begin a room spruce-up. What color works best where? Decorators know how to create special effects with color and lighting.

Light to Dark

Go from light to dark. Paint the first room you enter in a pale pastel; then paint the larger room in any one of the currently fashionable dark colors. This might be a darker version of the pale pastel color or a contrasting color. It's a soothing change that won't cost much.

Drab Furniture

Paint the walls and you'll be surprised how attractive everything else will become.

Try Something New

Don't be limited by convention. If your rooms are dark, change to light and vice versa. Either way the change will be an instant transformation.

Contrast

Paint one wall and paper another for contrast in color and texture.

Look Up

Don't be limited by the walls alone. A fresh new color on the ceiling will change your room quite a bit. A pale blue, for example, will give an entire room a lovely, cool feeling. Aqua is a wonderful color for the ceiling of porches. Pale peach or a hint of pink will cast a soft glow over the room. Use it in the dining room or bedroom.

Draw the Eye Upward

Once you've painted the ceiling, add a high shelf along one wall and fill it with baskets of greenery to draw the eye upward. Paint the molding in a slightly darker shade of the same pastel.

Lighting Impact

The way color looks is a result, in part, of lighting. Bounce light off the ceiling for indirect, soft lighting. To create intimacy in a dark room with paneled walls, paint the ceiling a mocha color and add low lighting along the floor. When lighting is bounced off warm pastel walls and ceiling, it warms the room. In a hot climate, bounce the light off pale blue walls.

Kitchen Lighting

Fluorescent lighting in a kitchen can be harsh. To warm the room, paint the ceiling in pale pastel.

From Tired to Terrific

A change of color is the quickest, easiest, and cheapest way to alter the look of an entire room. Use color to create different moods.

For Summer

Use red and white with accents of yellow. Choose a delicate floral pattern in these colors for wallpaper or fabric. Use the red for piping on white curtains. Or combine sun-drenched yellow with primrose blue and white. Edge the curtains with primrose.

Power Flower

This is a name often given to the yellow sunflower. For a strong impact use the design to paint the top of a round table or stool.

For Christmas

Spray paint old folding chairs gold. Stencil silver stars over the seats and backs. Spray paint pinecones and pineapples silver and display on the mantel.

Pure as Snow

If you're tired of all color, remove it and make everything white. Add pine wood accessories for a warm country theme. White is never dull.

Bright Accents

Containers of bright wildflowers do wonders to liven up a room. Use elegant flowers in simple, homey containers. An old jar can hold one strong flower such as a bright orange poppy. Fill mugs, water goblets, bottles, a creamer with small nosegays.

Rainbow of Ribbons

Tie back lace curtains with colorful ribbons. Change the color as often as you like. For a dinner party, stretch ribbons evenly spaced lengthwise across the table. Use colorful ribbons to tie around the napkins.

Check it Out

It's easy to add a touch of country to any room with accents of blue and white and red and white checked fabric. Combine big and little checks.

Little Changes, Big Results

Paint small areas such as baseboards, window and door trims, picture frames, shutters, cornices, shelf trim, and closet doors with accent colors.

Curtains

No need to change white curtains to get color in the room. Simply line them with a pretty provincial print and tie back with matching fabric.

Window Boxes

Attach window boxes to the outside where you want a touch of color inside. Then fill with plants that will grow above the window ledge and be visible from the inside. In this way you create color inside and out.

Daffodil Yellow

Traditionally, daffodils signify the arrival of spring in the Northeast. They're a reminder of how lovely the color yellow is in nature and how seldom it's used in interior design. Accents of yellow bring a splash of sunshine to otherwise dark areas of the house.

Sunny Hallway

A yellow printed wallpaper will make a hallway or entrance room positively glow, creating a warm and welcoming area.

Fabric Fancy

Combine a yellow floral print comforter with blue and white striped dust ruffle. Cover pillows with the print and add a full ruffle with the blue and white stripe. Repeat the fabric at the windows with the stripe as a valance. A blue carpet will go well with this bedroom ensemble.

Framed Prints

If you just want to add an accent touch of yellow to the bedroom, botanical prints of daffodils will do the trick. It's a nice springtime accent with blue, lavender, or green wallpaper and fabric.

Needlework Pillow

Roses have been overused as a theme for needlepoint, but a bunch of daffodils is new.

A Bouquet for Framing

If you like to do counted cross-stitch, a bouquet of daffodils would be suitable for framing in the kitchen or bathroom.

Stencil Border

Daffodils make a nice border around a kitchen, or on a recipe box if you feel less ambitious. Trace the flower from a book, a greeting card, or wrapping paper. Transfer it to stencil paper and cut out with a craft knife. Use this as a repeat for a springlike border or create a design on the drawers of a bureau.

Photo Fun

If you enjoy photographing nature, plan a series of florals. Choose the best and either enlarge or make color photocopies suitable for framing.

First Signs of Spring

Who can resist bringing the fresh daffys indoors as a reminder that each day brings warmer weather? Isn't it a shame the daffodil is so short-lived? Enjoy a simple bouquet while they last.

Tropical Colors for Summer

Go color crazy for the summer by using an array of shocking pink, vivid purple, tangerine orange, acid green, and other vibrant colors for a tropical look on a porch or patio. Then add a touch of black and white.

Pillows

Throw pillows that can be used indoors or out provide an inexpensive way to add color that's easy to put away at summer's end.

Placemats

Liven up the dining room or outdoor patio table with placemats and mismatched napkins in bright, splashy prints. Use interesting napkin rings with a tropical theme.

Black and White Relief

Use a ticking fabric for pillow accents. Or cover wicker seat cushions with black and white stripes, then add bright floral pillows. Use pure white chinaware with bright fabrics on the table. Fill a black ceramic vase with pure white freesia or carnations for the center of the table. Find interesting salt and pepper shakers, sugar bowl and creamer, and demitasse cups and saucers in black or white.

Architectural Interest

When decorating a room, start by identifying the room's important or interesting features. These features can become focal points in the room. Look for some architectural point of interest in a room as a departure. For example, if the molding is interesting, keep it natural to highlight it. If there is none, you can create it. There are many products on the market for creating architectural details such as columns, a mantelpiece, or elaborate molding.

Uninteresting Molding

If the molding is made of a lesser wood, paint it the same color as the ceiling.

Color Ideas

A deep green color can add interest to a high ceiling. Paint the molding a mauve color. Usually subtle contrasting colors work best, such as white with off-white. If you use two colors, try to keep them as close to the same color as possible. One might be a shade darker or lighter than the other.

Add Molding

If there is no molding in a room, add your own. Just buy the length you need, miter the corners with a miter box saw, and nail it in place.

Painting the Trim

Paint the ceiling molding with high gloss and use semi-gloss for chair rails. This is a good way to achieve some interest in space lacking architectural details.

Accessories

Reviving an Old Lamp

Tired of an old lamp? Update the shade with decorative trimmings. Each transformation will take less than one hour.

Romantic

Add a border of floral decals. Using white craft glue, attach each decal around the bottom edge of the shade. Create a 2-inch border by overlapping the flowers in one continuous band. This can also be done with cutouts from botanical prints, wrapping paper, or greeting cards.

Fabric Trim

If you have a scrap of material left over from making curtains or pillows, use it to decorate the lamp shade. Simply cut out the fabric—large flowers work best—and apply craft glue to the wrong side of each flower. Then, press them at random all over the shade. Space the flowers so they don't interfere with light coming through. For a child's room, cut out teddy bears, ducks, etc. from a juvenile print.

Eyelet Cover

Transform any shade with an elegant eyelet cover. Cut a strip of eyelet fabric to the same size as the widest circumference of the shade and add 3 inches to the height. Hem the top raw edge. With right sides facing, stitch the short edges of the eyelet together to form a tube. Turn it right side out and place it over the lamp shade. With a needle and thread, gather the fabric 2 inches down from the top and adjust the fabric on the shade. Light will shine through the eyelet, creating a pretty pattern. The edge of the eyelet should hang down slightly below the bottom edge of the shade to create a scalloped finish.

Stencil Border

Be your own designer with a simple country stencil, acrylic paint, and a brush (available in art stores). Position and tape the stencil to the front of the bottom edge of the shade and apply paint lightly to the cutout areas. Lift and reposition the stencil until you have completed a border all the way around. Use the same design to create a border around the top of the shade. This is a good way to recycle a lamp for a child's room.

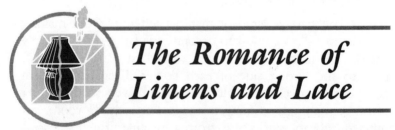

The Romance of Linens and Lace

I am a lifelong collector of vintage lace and linens, mostly from flea markets, from garage and estate sales, and from foraging through the attics of relatives. I love to hunt down lace in any form, from old petticoats to thin bands of remnants that might have edged an early christening dress.

Lace for Summer

Summertime is synonymous with lacy curtains slightly blowing in open windows, linen napkins on lovely white tablecloths, lace-edged pillowcases and sheets, and crocheted trims on guest towels.

A Hint of Luxury

You may not have a big armoire filled with edged pillow shams inherited from a loving grandmother, but there are ways to create small pleasures each time you open your linen closet or sit down to a meal, even if you're dining alone.

1. Tie a white satin ribbon around pure white pillowcases as they would have been in an Edwardian linen closet.
2. Tie a pale rose-colored ribbon around a few lace-edged hand towels and tuck a sachet under each.
3. Line the linen closet shelves with lavender-scented shelf paper.
4. Attach a simple white crocheted edging to plain white pillow shams for a contrast of textures.
5. If you are able, embroider a delicate ribbon or rosebuds along the edge of plain pillowcases.
6. Scour the thrift shops for petticoats to turn into curtains. My bathroom curtains were once the full underskirt of a wedding dress and my kitchen curtains were once lace-edged linen table runners.
7. Strips of new lace can be purchased by the yard. Dip it into hot tea for a few seconds to turn it into an old-world trim for bed linens and curtain swags.
8. Gather lace or sheer white curtains with tasseled silken cords or a large taffeta ribbon.

9. A cutwork doily or tea cloth softens any shelf, wooden table, or painted dresser and inspires a display of treasured items. One of my grandmother's cutwork tablecloths covers a small Shaker-style corner table in my living room. It's set on the diagonal so the cutwork corner dips over the edge. It holds antique picture frames, a plant in a wood-grain scoop and one of my rose-covered decoupage boxes filled with rose petals.

10. If you have a strip of lace or vintage linen too narrow to make a curtain, consider using it as a valance with a sheer café curtain below. Cover another window with a flat lace panel for light and privacy.

Space Makers

Folding screens are practical for solving certain room problems. Originally used in early homes to reduce drafts, this versatile accessory might serve the same purpose in an older home today. Screens are also functional as room dividers, to create a dining or work alcove, or to set off a temporary new baby's room. A screen can stand behind a desk or sofa. Use a screen as a backdrop for a seating arrangement with two chairs and a small table in front of it.

Victoriana

In the Victorian era, folding screens were quite elaborate, some made of gilded wood, others covered with decoupage or scrapbook items. Some were simple frames over which a pretty floral print was stretched. If you find one of these, even if it's not in perfect shape, consider yourself lucky. It will add distinction to any room.

A New Cover for an Old Screen

A folding screen needn't be old to be interesting. Look for them at second-hand shops or yard sales. Repaint, paper, or cover with linen. They can provide the perfect area on which to display artistically arranged photos and momentos.

Ready to Finish

Unfinished furniture stores often sell wood screens. Some have decorative panels. These are perfect for a contrasting paint treatment. You might also cover the panels with wallpaper or fabric to match your walls or curtains and upholstered furniture.

Mail Order

The Sears catalog has unfinished, plain screens in various sizes. Since these are fairly plain-looking, add interest in the following way. Paint or apply a printed wallpaper background to each panel. Using botanical greeting cards, postcards, or calendar prints, space and arrange them in a pattern on the screen. Then, use thin velvet or grosgrain ribbon to frame each one. To simulate a gallery display, run the ribbon down the full length of each panel between each "framed" picture so they appear to be hanging.

Do-It-Yourself with Doors

Make an interesting one-of-a-kind screen with refurbished old doors or narrow, hollow-core doors and two-way hinges. Add molding if desired and apply a painting technique such as sponging or pickling, or hand-rub with wood stain.

The Artful Way

Another way to make your own screen is with artist's stretchers. They come in various sizes and simply snap together. Attach the sections with brass hinges where the panels meet. Stretch fabric over each panel and secure by stapling to the back of each frame. If you want the back to be finished as well, cover with a contrasting fabric and hide the staples with a decorative braid or ribbon glued all around.

More for Your Money

Screens can also be made from plywood, foamboard, fiberboard, Sheetrock, or blueboard. Hinges for the light materials can be made from strong cloth tape. Most screens only require two hinges, one attached about a third of the way from the top and another one-third up from the bottom. For best results, look for two-way hinges.

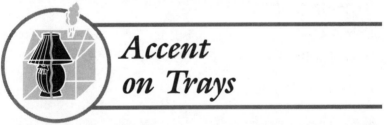

Accent on Trays

As a decorative accessory, trays can go way beyond the utilitarian uses for which they were originally intended.

Frame a Collection

Arrange a collection of shells within the framework of a pretty tray and they will take on an artistic quality. If you have a glass-top table, a pretty tray sets off the collection that might simply fade into the carpet or floor below.

Display a Tray

There are many different types of trays. Stand a particularly pretty tray on end over a mantel or on a shelf. If the tray doesn't have any decoration but is painted a nice color, use it as the background against which to set a vase of flowers or a figurine.

Bring an Old Tray to Life

Now and then I find an old metal tray at a garage sale. A coat of spray paint brings it back to life instantly and a faux finish will turn it into a decorative accessory. There are marbleizing kits that make this technique easy enough for anyone to master. Sponge painting is quite effective for this item. I prefer decoupage and love to look for beautiful botanical prints to cut out and apply to items like this. If you paint a tray white and apply several coats of satin varnish it will look like ivory.

Organize Clutter

Trays are great for organizing small items that create clutter. Use an elegant silver tray to hold ordinary items, such as spools of thread and scissors or items that belong on a desk. I use a narrow, ornate silver sugar cube tray to hold paper clips on my desk.

Hold the Mail

If your front hallway table becomes cluttered with the daily mail, a pretty tray might be just the thing. The mail will still be visible, but somehow it will seem more orderly.

All Bottled Up

Use a pretty tray—silver is nice—to hold unusual perfume bottles and containers of cosmetics on a dressing table or in the bathroom.

Add Color

Colorful plastic trays of no great monetary value lend a cheerful note to the kitchen counter. Arrange fresh fruit on a bright orange or lemon yellow tray. Use one of these trays to hold a bright teapot with unmatched yard-sale sugar and creamer.

Center of Attention

Papier-mâché trays or those painted with a tole border are making a comeback. Place one on end in a bookcase and stand two or three leather-bound books on each side. Add a cherished piece of chinaware or a small vase filled with fresh flowers in front of the tray between the books.

In Disguise

If you have a nicely shaped tray but the design isn't particularly great, group a bunch of interesting objects on top of it, using the shape as a border to contain the grouping.

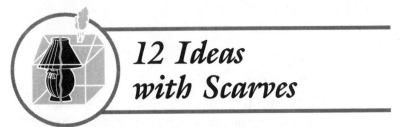

12 Ideas with Scarves

What do designer scarves have to do with decorating for the home? If you're on a limited budget, you can make small changes, like covering a pillow with a beautiful silk scarf, that add high style at very little cost.

Valance

Long silk scarves will drape easily over a curtain rod to create a soft valance. If you have a wide window, drape one in the center and tie two more with a decorative knot at each side edge.

Seat Cushions

Use oversized cotton scarves, such as bandanas, to cover seat cushions. You may have to combine two, one on top and one underneath. If you use two different colors it can be more interesting than a pillow covered with the same color on the top and underside.

Pillows

Make throw pillows for any area of the home. If you want elegance, use silk or velvet; for outdoors use a polyester/cotton blend in bright tropical colors.

Lamp Shade

Long, thin chiffon scarves are great for a romantic look. Use a pretty pattern to drape over a lamp shade. The light will shine through and create soft lighting.

Kitchen Stools

If you have wooden bar stools in your kitchen, for example, pad the top with quilt batting and stuffing and cover each with a cotton scarf. Pull the edges to the underside and staple all around.

Napkins

Cotton scarves make wonderful oversized napkins, especially for outdoors or for buffet dining. Give everyone a different pattern or use the same pattern in different colors.

Tablecloth

For an interesting tablecloth, make a patchwork of same-size scarves stitched together to create the size needed.

Dining Chair Seat

A scarf is just the right size for covering the seat of a dining chair. Remove the screws from the underside. The seat will lift off easily. Remove the old seat cover or just add the scarf right over it, staple or tack to the underside, and replace the whole thing. Each seat can match or be different. This is an easy way to change the look from winter to summer, then back again in the fall.

Table Combo

Cover a side table with a plain tablecloth, then top it with a pretty patterned scarf in a color to match.

Pillow Shams

Use two delicate scarves to make pillow shams for the bedroom. If the scarves have a scalloped edge, all the better.

Café Curtains

Since all edges of a scarf are finished, it's a cinch to turn scarves into café curtains. Just turn one edge down, press and stitch, then hang. Silk or rayon scarves will create a curtain with soft folds. A polyester or cotton scarf will have more body. Either way, taking them down, washing, and rehanging is a breeze.

Apron

For a pretty apron in minutes, stitch a piece of 1-inch-wide grosgrain ribbon, long enough to tie around your waist, to one edge of a cotton scarf.

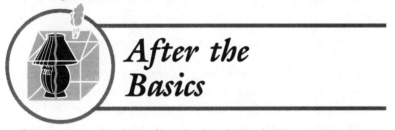

After the Basics

Once a room has been furnished with the basics, accessorizing is an ongoing process that lends liveliness and interest to a room. An accessory is either functional or pleasant to look at. Those that are functional should work easily and properly. Those that are aesthetic should make us happy when we look at them.

Choosing the Right Things

Don't buy an object just to fill a space. When you see the "right" thing it will speak to you.

Easy to Change

Accessories aren't permanent. It's fun to try things in different spots. You may buy something for one place and find that it looks better elsewhere. If you fall in love with an item you'll undoubtedly find a place for it.

Combining Objects

Combine shapes, colors, and sizes for an interesting grouping of different objects.

Interesting Corner

If you have a particularly interesting corner, use a dramatic object to focus attention on this area.

Plants for Liveliness

Lighten up a room with plants and flowers. For a garden effect, group several plants of different sizes and heights.

A Touch of Humor

Interesting, even irreverent objects add humor in an otherwise serious setting. A friend of mine who happens to be an artist collects frogs as well as English souvenir tins, antique mechanical toys, paintings, and sculpture by other artists he admires. The small frogs, placed throughout the house, are humorous and fun to come upon.

One Important Piece

Sometimes one important accessory is all it takes to create interest in an otherwise ordinary room. Even if you don't know what is needed, you almost can't miss with an Early American folk art piece. It will provide aesthetic pleasure with the added plus of being a good, long-term investment. And you might like to know that primitive folk paintings are coming into their own as well. They are still affordable and are increasing in value every year.

Low Tech

When it comes to functional accessories, almost every home includes high-tech equipment. A home office is more interesting when your desk holds pretty as well as functional items. Find interesting low-tech objects such as baskets to hold accessories (tapes or computer paper, for example).

Playful Scene

Fun accessories add a bit of whimsy. Top an adult dresser or side table with a little bowl of colorful marbles or a child's toy. My mother always had a rag doll sitting in a rocker in the living room long after there were any children living in her house. It made the room seem young at heart.

Shopping the Five-and-Ten

I have a confession to make. I love five-and-ten-cent stores. Not discount chains that sell everything from dishtowels to furniture, but the old-fashioned Woolworth's and Lamston's that I frequented as a child. While worldly travelers know exactly where to get the best whatnots, accessories, and gizmos in every city in the world, I am a five-and-ten aficionada. Really good five-and-tens are predictable. Everything is where it's supposed to be and you know you'll find what you're looking for and the price will be right. But I like the fact that I can find exactly what I wasn't looking for as well. In this regard the five-and-ten is like a yard sale. It offers the element of anticipation.

Savvy Shopping

The five-and-tens keep up with trends in their own way, but you have to be sharp to spot a good, trendy buy that doesn't look cheap. While there have always been inexpensive copies of expensive items, the five-and-ten usually has copies of the copies. And once you take something out of this environment, it tends to look better. For example, a "faux tortoise" plastic frame around a decent beveled mirror might look pretty good surrounded by your own furnishings. Who would imagine it's not the real thing?

Good Buys

Aside from the everyday necessities such as sewing notions, toiletries, and party favors, there are special things to find. Outdoor furniture such as lounge chairs and folding tables are usually good buys. And those little plastic tables with the legs you insert are perfect for the patio. Picture frames, baskets, and artificial flowers are mainstays of the five-and-ten. But if you haven't wandered through the housewares department you might not think to look for curtains and curtain rods, placemats, pot holders, cloth napkins, and such here.

A Little Trim Goes a Long Way

Look for the plainest you can find, then add your own trim. For example, silk braid makes custom curtains expensive. Buy the trim in a decorator fabric shop and add it to sheer five-and-ten curtains. No one will be the wiser. A strip of eyelet or grosgrain ribbon added to the edge of plain, inexpensive towels makes them pretty enough for a shower gift.

Lamps

Candle lamps with marble bases are popular in boutiques. The five-and-ten has its own version. Not badly designed, it's basic and functional and costs $20, not $45–$60 for the next best version and $120 for the real McCoy. Whatever the latest trend in lamps, whether it's a goose-neck or a halogen, the five-and-ten has a cheap version.

Seasonal Needs

The basic goal of a five-and-ten is to supply items that we need when we need them. But they also respond to seasonal needs, so it pays to plan ahead. You may think the aisle that holds closet organizers is always stocked no matter when you decide to clean up your act. But if you're serious about filling your closet with perfectly matched pink hangers and getting just the right garment bags, the best supplies are stocked in the spring.

Not All Five-and-Tens Are Alike

Some five-and-tens "specialize" in order to respond to the neighborhood. For example, one store may have a terrific plant department while another might carry pet supplies. Maybe this is because there isn't a florist nearby the one, or the other store is close to a pet shop.

Out-of-Towners

When you take a trip to another town, check out the five-and-ten. Approach it as you would a yard sale. Look at the merchandise with an open mind. Can this rag rug really be only $9.95 and could I get away with it in my bathroom? If you have a good eye you'll recognize a good buy and realize that once it's in your home it may look as good as a more expensive version of the same item.

Not Always Cheaper

A word of caution. There is an assumption that everything here is cheaper, but it's not necessarily so. Get to know your five-and-ten. There's always the chance of stumbling upon something truly sensational.

Decorating with Quilts

A survey by the Hobby Industry Association indicates that 77% of all U.S. households now contain at least one hobbyist. Quilting is the number one craft, with over 3 million quilters in this country. Most quilts are made to cover beds, but more and more quilters are displaying them on walls. Decorating with quilts is a relatively affordable way to enhance a room. The patterns, colors, and craftsmanship render them worthy of hanging as you might a painting.

How to Hang a Quilt

There are many options for hanging a quilt.

1. On the top back of your quilt, hand sew a 4-inch strip of fabric such as muslin or a piece of backing fabric to create a channel and slide a flat wooden lathe or dowel through it. Put eye hooks into the ends of the dowel and attach to cup hooks inserted into the wall.

2. Another option for hanging a quilt is to sew a strip of Velcro to each side of the quilt back with corresponding strips attached to the wall.

3. Walker Systems, Inc. is a company that has devised ways to hang quilts on any wall. They have three different methods using adjustable bars, a rod support system, or clips. If you are interested the company will send information free of charge. Write to Walker Systems, Inc., 250 South Lake Ave., Duluth, MN 55802.

Where to Hang a Quilt

Strong sunlight will fade a quilt. Keep away from radiators and out of damp environments that can cause mildew. Depending on size and color, a quilted wallhanging will fit with any style of decorating. While quilts are most often thought of as country style, the designs can look surprisingly contemporary. A quilt will add warmth and charm to any room.

Miniature Magic

If you'd like to make a certain quilt pattern but can't commit the time to making a full-size quilt, consider a miniature. These can be any size, but a doll's crib quilt is very attractive for framing and hanging. The idea of making quick quilts in a weekend has really caught on.

A Variation on a Theme

Choose a quilt pattern that you like and make a 12 by 12-inch square for framing. This is a quick and easy way to create textured art and you can quilt a small square on your lap.

Amish Quilts

These quilts have always been prized and they are still the most interesting, and the most expensive to buy. The designs are simple but elegant and the colors distinctive. Dark greens, purples, blues, deep red, and black are the dominant shades.

Pure Elegance

White-on-white quilts are quite beautiful, with the interest coming from the stitch pattern. It's rare to find these quilts in good condition, but you can make one by using a traditional pattern, such as the Log Cabin, with different shades of neutrals for a contemporary room.

Classic American Design

Nothing is appreciated more than an Early American country quilt. This piece of American folk art has stood the test of time and reveals much about our country. The patterns, the workmanship, the colors, and the quilting designs are a part of our heritage. Modern-day quiltmakers still find these patterns worth re-creating and are discovering the wide range of beautiful fabrics that make the designs look fresh and new.

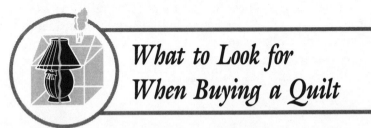

What to Look for
When Buying a Quilt

Quilts add warmth and country charm to any area of the home. No longer used only as bed covering, we find quilts on walls, used as curtains and valances, and made into pillows. With the rising cost of good antique quilts, the market has expanded for new quilts. Having written several books on quilts and quilting, I am often asked how one recognizes a good buy in quilts, old or new. A quilt, like most folk art, is a good collectable and over time will only go up in value.

What Can You Afford?

Decide what you can afford and don't buy anything you don't love just because the price is low. There aren't any real bargains, but quilts are still affordable. However, you get what you pay for. Chances are, if the quilt is exceptionally cheap, the design and workmanship are of poor quality.

Patchwork

Patchwork quilts have always been considered more valuable than appliqué quilts, even though you can find beautiful appliqué quilts, both old and new. When showing you a pieced quilt, a dealer might point out the many thousands of squares that make up a quilt. However, if they are stitched in a shoddy manner and there is no handquilting around each square, or the design isn't pleasing, the fact that someone pieced them together on a machine is of no particular value. Look to see that the quilt pieces were carefully measured and sewn accurately with all seams and corners meeting properly.

Appliqué

Machine-stitched appliqué is not as attractive or valuable as hand-sewn appliqué. This would only be found on a new quilt, as old quilts were always done strictly by hand. A machine-appliquéd quilt should be less expensive, however, and can be just as pretty if you are simply looking for a decorative and practical element for your bed.

Consider Color

Antique quilts are made of all-cotton fabrics that were not colorfast. This is why the colors of an old quilt have that wonderfully soft, faded quality. The colors of newer quilts tend to be brighter. If the colors are bright the quilt is newer and was probably made with a blend of polyester and cotton, which is practical for everyday use and should be less expensive.

Design Decisions

Patchwork patterns are made up of squares and triangles that form geometric shapes. These shapes are used to create blocks that are joined to make up the patchwork top of the quilt. The traditional designs used years ago have been copied, revised, and reproduced faithfully by modern-day quilters using up-to-date fabrics. These are still the most sought after in new as well as old quilts. They include such patterns as Log Cabin, Irish Chain, Bear Claw, Turkey Tracks, and Around the World or Sunshine and Shadow. Star patterns in all variations are among the most popular.

Familiar appliqué designs include Rose of Sharon, Flower Basket, Teacup, and Tulips. Flowers are always in demand.

Quality Quilts

Quilting is the most important element of a quality quilt. The pieced top, a layer of batting, and a piece of fabric called the backing are stitched together with small, evenly spaced stitches. This is the quilting. The more stitches to the inch, the more valuable a quilt. An antique quilt will usually be covered with an overall pattern of evenly spaced stitches. These quilts were often done at quilting bees where several women worked on the project together and the amount of time spent was of no consequence.

Identifying New Quilts

Newer quilts generally don't have as much quilting as old quilts and the stitching is often confined to following the seam lines of the joined pieces. New quilts often have large borders with the pieced design in the center of the quilt. The borders are then filled with a quilting pattern such as swirls or a winding vine and leaves or a simple grid.

Making Your Own

If you can't afford the size and design of a quilt you need for your room, you might like to know how easy it is to make your own. If you can sew a straight line on a sewing machine you can make a perfect patchwork quilt. Quiltmaking is the most popular craft in America today and there are literally hundreds of good quilting books on the market for every skill level. *The Weekend Quilt* (St. Martin's Press) is my most popular, with nineteen quilts to piece in a weekend.

Creative Ways with Quilts

Occasionally you may find a quilt that is too damaged to use as a bedcover. There are many great ways to use the salvageable parts. Decorating with quilts adds interest to any home because there is such a wide range of colors and textures from which to choose.

Fitted Covers

Use a geometric quilt to make fitted mattress covers for daybeds in a den or teen's room. Choose a simple patchwork pattern and a color combination to suit the room. This is a good way to recycle parts of a large bed quilt.

Headboard

Another good use for a fairly large damaged quilt is making an upholstered headboard.

Pillows

If you have an old quilt that isn't in good enough condition to use on a bed or as a wallhanging, cut it up for throw pillows. In fact, if you can find pieces of quilted tops, sometimes available at craft shows, you can make a variety of good-looking pillow shams.

Animal Pillows

Make country farm animal pillows. Patterns are available in books and from McCall's, Butterick, and Simplicity.

Draperies

Make quilted draperies from floral fabrics. This is a good way to add insulation over the windows in cold months.

Accessories from Remnants

Use small quilted pieces of fabric to cover desk accessories such as a date book or pencil holder.

Letter Holder

Stitch quilted pot holder squares to a piece of fabric backing, such as felt, and hang from a wooden dowel in the kitchen. Use the pockets to hold mail.

Quilted Wreath

A grapevine wreath can be decorated with quilted fabric leaves and grapes. To make grapes, cover balls of stuffing with fabric circles and wire together in clusters.

Placemats

Quilted placemats are easy to make in different patchwork or appliqué patterns for the holidays. It's a great way to use up scraps.

Quick and Easy

Strip quilting is an easy method for quick quilting. You just stitch 1–2-inch strips of fabric together, then cut into equal units, such as 4-inch squares, and arrange in a pattern for a quilt top, pillow, placemats, runner, etc.

Shower Curtain

For the bathroom, quick-stitch a patchwork shower curtain from large squares of fabric. Waverly has a shell pattern that is perfect when combined with solid squares.

Frame It

Make a quilted frame for a wall-mounted bathroom mirror. Cover strips of wood with batting and quilted fabric and attach to the wall around the mirror.

Tabletops

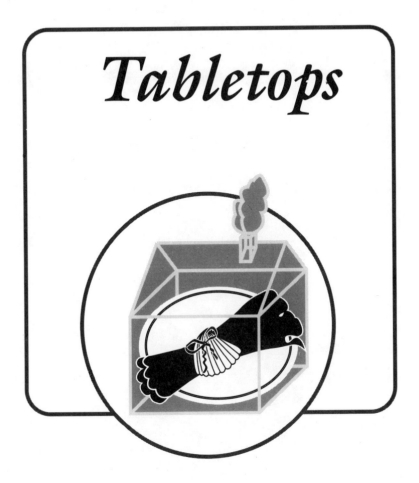

Napkins and Holders

It's ecologically smart to use cloth napkins. For everyday use, there are easy-care napkins, but for party fare it's always fun to dress up the table with pretty napkins and creative rings.

Cheap and Serviceable

For everyday use I buy dishtowels on sale, cut them in half, and hem the raw edges to make my own napkins. My mother gave me this idea years ago and I buy different colors every time dishtowels are on sale. I bought red and white plaid for the holidays and black and white to use with white placemats. Blue and white checks and plaids are perfect for summer meals in the backyard.

For Picnics

For picnics, children's parties, and outdoor barbecues use washcloths. You can buy different colors and toss them in the washing machine after the meal. Buy red, white, and blue for a Fourth of July party.

For Buffets

Buffets often involve balancing a plate of food on one's lap. Oversized napkins work best. Buy remnants of different floral prints to make them 22–24 inches square. Edge each one with grosgrain ribbon to match a color in the print. When you have a party, tie with a ribbon and set at each place. This makes a table dressy with little effort or expense.

Nature's Way

Tie twigs around rolled napkins and insert a leaf or two for a fall or Thanksgiving dinner. A large leaf is another nice way to encircle a rolled napkin. Pin to secure.

By the Seashore

String ribbon through a shell and tie around a napkin for a seaside theme, or a seafood dinner.

Dye It Better

If your napkins are too soiled for use, dye them a pretty color. It's easy. Just dunk them into a bath of fabric dye. Experiment by holding parts of the napkin in the dye for different lengths of time for a strié affect. Or tie the napkins in knots and insert in the dye bath for a tie-dyed effect.

China

Many of us have fine chinaware, perhaps handed down from other generations, but we're reluctant to use it for fear of breakage. Good news! This needn't be a worry any longer. If you have an incomplete set of your grandmother's dishes and want to find the missing pieces, you can do so through a service that will replace any pattern or piece of china, crystal, or silverware no matter how antique or obscure.

Bob Page, president and founder of a company called Replacements, Ltd., will find the most obsolete, active, and inactive china, crystal, fine bone, and flatware. He stocks over 1 million pieces of more than 25,000 patterns in his vast warehouse. He says, "Collecting antique china is an act of love...and patience. But the rewards of creating lovely tabletops are worth it."

Advice for Collectors

To determine the quality of a piece of china, hold it up to the light to check for translucence. The more translucent, the better the quality.

Tips for Preserving Antique Tableware

1. Always wash it by hand with a mild soap or detergent. Avoid abrasives that can ruin the finish on fine china.
2. Use a rubber mat to cushion the sink.
3. Use plate racks to stand plates up, or place a piece of flannel or paper towel between each plate when stacking. This prevents scratching.
4. Hang cups separately on a rack. Do not stack.
5. For sparkling crystal, use ammonia in the wash and add a little vinegar to the rinse water.
6. Sterling flatware improves with use. Don't soak. Wash immediately after use.

If a piece of fine china is broken or marred, don't despair. A replacement is only a phone call or letter away. If you don't know the name of your pattern, send a photocopy of the front and back of the item and make notations about colors and markings. Contact Replacements, Ltd., 302 Gallimore Dairy Rd., Greensboro, NC 27409-9723, telephone (919) 668-2064.

Romance by Candlelight

Candles make a table glow with romance. They create a special ambience and the more the better. I always look for glasses, snifters, and goblets of all sizes and shapes when I go to yard sales, flea markets, and antique stores. Even when I'm on vacation, the first thing I buy is a glass vase to hold a candle in my room or rented house.

Votives

These short, fat little candles should always be bunched together in their own containers for impact. To make them festive, wrap leaves around them and tie with twine or secure with a pin.

Plain Wrapper

Wrap a piece of muslin or burlap around a tall glass to hold a fat candle. Tie a piece of rope or twine around the middle and secure with a decorative knot.

Hurricane Substitutes

For an inexpensive hurricane lamp, use a snifter or glass vase. These are easy to find in the five-and-ten or a pharmacy with a housewares department. I have even found interesting glass vases with etched designs in the supermarket. They are perfectly fine for patio dining.

Living in a Fish Bowl

A goldfish bowl will hold one large candle or several votive candles. It's a terrific shape and size for a dramatically lit centerpiece.

Fruity Statement

Scoop out a hole from the center of red or green apples and insert thin, short candles. They're great at Christmastime. For the fall, use tiny pumpkins and gourds.

Thanksgiving Table Tips

You may only be thinking about preparing the Thanksgiving dinner. But sooner or later you'll get around to the fun of setting the table. Napkins and napkin rings will add a fashion statement to your table.

All Tied Up

Use beautiful ribbons in different fall colors to tie printed or solid-color napkins in autumn shades. A country patchwork quilt is the perfect table covering.

A Fruity Theme

Fruit is a nice theme for the Thanksgiving table. It's a welcome change from a centerpiece of flowers. To go with this theme use napkins in a beautiful fruit print. It's easy to make them. Cut a square of 18-inches and hem all around. Choose one of the colors in the print for your tablecloth.

All-American Theme

While we usually think of red, white, and blue for the Fourth of July, using just red or blue with white will give the table a country style for this most American of holidays. If you have the time and inclination to make your own tablecloth, a stencil pattern of random stars on a solid fabric background is an easy way to create a unique and striking table.

Unfinished Project

I like a country theme for this holiday and reserve the glitter and sparkle for Christmas. If you've started a patchwork quilt and have only gotten as far as piecing the top, use it for a tablecloth in the meantime. Place a piece of thin cotton quilt batting or padding between the table and fabric.

Dyeing to Know

It's easy to color plain wooden rings with fabric dye. Dilute the dye in boiling water according to package directions and submerge the rings for several minutes. Remove and let dry on a paper towel.

Recycled

For napkin rings that cost nothing, cut paper towel tubes into equal widths and cover with pretty ribbon, fabric, or paper.

A Ring of Fruit

Use artificial fruit such as a small cluster of grapes wired around each napkin. Or intertwine grape vines around the napkins.

Fourth of July Party

For a July Fourth party, choose food as well as tableware that complements the red, white, and blue theme.

Table Cover

Remove the sticks from inexpensive parade flags and stitch the flags together to make placemats or a banner to place down the center of the table as a runner.

Table Setting

Cover the table with red and blue spatter-painted canvas (could be a painter's drop cloth). Fill a blue spatterware pitcher with red carnations. Place a red napkin on each blue spatterware plate. Fill a bright red bowl with red grapes or blueberries for the centerpiece.

Patriotic Table

Buy a patriotic patchwork quilt to hang or use as a table cover at a July Fourth party. Or make a red and white or blue and white patchwork cover for the occasion.

Not for Stitchers

If sewing isn't your thing, stencil a traditional quilt pattern in red, white, and blue on an artist's canvas or a piece of plywood.

Stars and Stripes Forever

Throughout the year collect all sorts of tabletop items adorned with stars or stripes or in red, white, and blue colors to use for your July Fourth table. Yard sales are a good source and you'll be surprised how creative a table you'll set with a bunch of mismatched but interesting items with a theme.

Flowers, Vegetables, and Fruit

Fill a basket with fresh, polished apples, a mushroom basket with bright red tomatoes, a white bowl with plump strawberries, and a pitcher with blue cornflowers. That's all you'll need for delicious decorations.

Napkins and Napkin Holders

Use blue and white checked dishtowels for the napkins at a barbecue and tie each with red streamers. Attach sticker stars to the ends of the ribbons.

Paint Your Own Tablecloth

Use plain white shelf paper and Magic Markers to make a giant flag for a table cover.

Dress
It Up

Custom Fits

It's easy to customize plain, inexpensive household items that would cost a great deal more if you had them specially made. In many cases you might not be able to get exactly what you want unless you make it yourself.

Window Covers

Buy plain white balloon shades to fit your windows. Then add a 3-inch ruffle of a printed fabric to match your upholstered pieces. If your balloon shade is made of printed fabric, add a ruffle of stripes or polka dots down the sides, across the bottom edge, and between the panels where the fabric is drawn up. Make matching pillows for the sofa.

Sheets

Buy contrasting sheets, such as a blue and white plaid and a blue and white pinstripe. Combine them for curtains, tiebacks, cushion covers, and tablecloths in your kitchen.

Mix and Match

Use different large and small prints, stripes, and checks and combine the fabrics for the fronts and backs of pillows, ruffles, and cording. Be sure all the fabric comes from one manufacturer so the colors match even though the prints are different.

Stenciled Sisal

Stencil a large pattern around a sisal rug. Or use fabric dye to "paint" every other square of a checkerboard sisal rug. Dissolve the dye in boiling water and apply it with a sponge brush. The dye will seep through to the underside, so do this outdoors or on many layers of newspaper to absorb the water.

Lace Border

Cut scalloped paper doilies in half and glue them end to end on top of wallpaper around a room to create a lacy border where the wall and ceiling meet. This treatment is nice in a young girl's room or bathroom.

Don't Throw It Away

Before you throw away that plastic bottle or cardboard container, stop! Recycle and create an interesting accessory at the same time. There are lots of throwaways that can be turned into useful and pretty containers.

For Your Desk

Paint a Band-Aid or aspirin tin, then glue stamps all over it at random. Spray a coat of varnish over all and you have a pretty stamp or paper clip holder. Glue an artificial flower to the top of a plastic traveling toothbrush box to hold pencils on your desk.

Plant Proof

Fill an ordinary plastic pail with an ivy plant. Decorate the outside of the container with trailing ivy decals to look like the real thing. The weatherproof plant holder is perfect for the patio.

Hold Everything

Paper paint buckets cost about fifty cents and are great as catchalls. Spray paint them and decorate with decals or cutout flowers from wrapping paper, or trim with decorative braid. Use them to hold tennis balls, cooking utensils, balls of yarn, or scraps of fabric. For the children, decorate them with Disney characters cut from self-adhesive Con-Tact paper and line them on a shelf to hold mittens, hats, toys, puzzle pieces, and underwear within easy reach.

Favorite Photo

Paint an old bread board, mount a favorite snapshot in the middle, and decorate the surrounding area with pretty cutout flowers and butterflies. Edge the picture with a band of ribbon and hang for an inexpensive frame.

Bright Storage

For the kids' room, cover sturdy cardboard boxes with bright self-adhesive paper and use them for toys and outdoor gear. This will encourage cleanup and keep the room looking neat and cheerful.

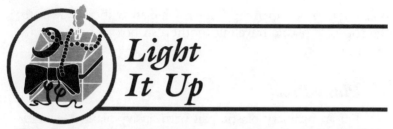

Light It Up

Tiny Christmas tree lights can be used all year long to add a little light or sparkle where needed.

Cupboards

Use a string of clear lights concealed in an armoire or cupboard to light up a collection of plates. Hide the cord behind the plates and they will glow from behind.

Bookcases

Books create dark areas that will benefit from discreet lighting. Run a string of lights behind the books to bring this area to life.

Potted Trees

Wind small, clear lights around and through the branches of potted trees such as ficus, especially if they are located in a dark corner. At night the lighted tree will give off just enough sparkle, especially when you don't want to light up the entire room. This is nice lighting for a party.

Outdoors

Place a string of tiny lights along a fence around a deck or patio, or string them around a table umbrella for nighttime glitter.

In a Bowl

If you're having a party, fill a glass punch bowl with a handful of lights and surround it with greenery. The lights will glow from behind the greens for a subtle centerpiece. Hide the cord behind the table.

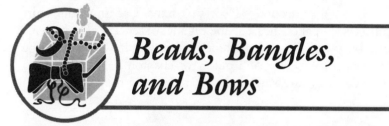

Beads, Bangles, and Bows

Pretty fabric bows, upholstery braid, tassels, and buttons add a touch of color and detail that gives a finishing touch to ordinary items.

Bows

Tie up a canopy with printed chintz fabric bows at each corner of the bed. If the canopy is made of a filmy white gauze, it will look sensational with a floral or overall print fabric to match accents in the room.

Slipcover Details

Edge the bottom of your slipcover with fat cording covered in contrasting fabric, or use decorative upholstery braid to trim the edge. A scalloped edge added to the bottom of a slipcover lends an interesting detail as well.

Bedeck the Fireplace

Hand paint a graceful ribbon around the fireplace. Draw it with a soft pencil, then fill in with acrylic or oil paint. If you don't feel confident enough to do this, use a delicate stencil design.

Buttoned Up

Rather than a zipper closure, use large, interesting buttons evenly spaced across the top of a throw pillow cover. Buttons can be used to decorate all sorts of items. Use tiny white shirt buttons to make a heart shape on a lacy sachet. Large buttons can be glued around a framed photograph. Use one large button in the center of a pillow or cushion. Glue buttons to the edge of a dressing table or around the mirror.

Ribbon Madness

Ribbons are used for decorative touches, for camouflage, or in place of fabric. They offer an inexpensive solution to many decorating problems and it's fun to think of new and creative projects using ribbons.

Camouflage

If you have an unsightly heating duct or other exposed pipe in your house, decorate it with bright colored paint and turn it into a Maypole. Take different colored ribbons and hang them from the top all around to make the pipe festive.

Curtains

Use ribbons in place of curtains. Tie strips of ribbon, cut to the same length, close together onto a rod so the ends stick up and create a bit of fringe. When the window is open the ribbons gently blow. Light filters in, yet there is privacy. This is a good way to create a colorful café curtain in a child's room.

Woven Art

Ribbons can also be used to make a woven sachet or pillow. Cut a piece of backing fabric to the desired size. Next, cut equal lengths of ribbon to fit across the width of the pillow. Place the ribbons side by side on the fabric and pin each end to the backing. Cut lengths of ribbon to weave in and out lengthwise across the pillow. Pin ribbons in place and machine stitch the raw ribbon ends around the pillow top. Cut a piece of pretty satin or velvet for the back and with right sides facing and raw edges aligned, stitch around three sides and four corners. Turn the pillow right side out and stuff. Slipstitch the opening closed.

Tie One On

Use ribbons as decorative ties to hold curtains to a rod. Cut equal lengths of about 8 to 10 inches and fold each strip in half lengthwise. Attach each folded ribbon to the back of the top edge of the curtain so they are evenly spaced. Tie to the curtain rod in a bow or with a knot, leaving the ribbon ends loose. Use matching ribbons as tiebacks. This treatment looks particularly nice when delicate sheer or lace curtains are combined with green or rose ribbons.

Decorate an Afghan

Decorate a loosely knit or crocheted afghan. Weave ¼-inch-wide satin ribbon in and out of the stitches at evenly spaced intervals.

Black and White All Over

Ribbons come in all different widths, designs, and finishes such as satin, grosgrain, and velvet. I'm partial to 1-inch-wide grosgrain with black and white stripes or polka dots. They create a bold graphic design when stitched to the edge of stark white towels.

Making It Personal

Personalize towels, linens, or a child's bathmat with a quick-stitch appliqué, ribbons, or lace.

Bathtime Fun

Add simple appliqués to a child's towel and bathmat to make bathtime more fun. Choose primary colors for the towels and bathmat and bright colored scraps for the appliqués. It's easy to create your own designs from simple shapes. A child's book can provide a colorful beach ball, a car, a farm animal, or a train to trace for a pattern. Pin the appliqué in place and zigzag stitch with your sewing machine around the edges.

Blossoming Towels

Buy plain hand towels and decorate them with floral appliqués cut from fabric. Apply them with fusible webbing (such as Stitch Witchery) or zigzag stitch around the raw edges. Add a fancy trim such as satin ribbon, eyelet, or rickrack and you have a beautiful gift for a fraction of the cost of buying it finished.

From Plain to Fancy

You can add your own touch to a variety of purchased items, such as the edges of pillowcases, napkins, or tablecloths; the pocket of a bathrobe, apron, or child's overalls; curtains; and decorative throw pillows. Turn a plain hanky into a fancy one in minutes with a beautiful lace trim or appliqué.

A Treasure from Trash

Turn plain, green paper berry baskets from the supermarket into handsome containers for holding all sorts of items. These baskets come in three or four sizes, so they will hold a variety of shapes. When covered with pretty paper and varnished with a shiny finish they look like fine ceramic cachepots and they are waterproof.

Paper Disguise

Use wallpaper, wrapping paper, or self-adhesive decorative paper to cover the berry basket. You'll also need white glue, a sponge, scissors, a pencil, and clear spray varnish.

Use the basket to trace and cut a piece of paper for each side, inside and out, as well as the bottom. Cut each piece slightly larger than the actual tracing to allow for overlap at the edges. Glue each piece to the basket. The bottom of the inside and underside should be glued last. Let dry for a half hour, then spray all sides, inside and out, with clear varnish. This will take minutes to dry and should be repeated three or four times. The varnish gives the basket a high gloss. It will be sturdy, waterproof, and chinalike in appearance. Suddenly a scrap material becomes elegant!

Planters

The smaller berry containers will fit neatly on a windowsill and can be used to hold small plants or herbs. Group several to create a centerpiece.

Desk Set

Choose a graphic or geometric pattern to cover the baskets for use on a desk set. Black and white checkerboard self-adhesive paper is shiny and waterproof. No varnish necessary.

A Great Notion

Use a calico-like print to cover baskets for holding spools of thread or other sewing notions. Trim the edge with rick-rack or grosgrain ribbon.

Baby Shower

Cover one of the baskets with wrapping paper in a baby theme and fill it with cotton balls, powder, etc. to take with a shower gift or to the hospital. Or fill with a small African violet plant and choose matching paper to wrap the berry basket.

Cosmetic Container

Wrap several of these baskets with leftover wallpaper from your bathroom or bedroom. Line them on a shelf or place in a convenient spot in the bathroom to hold cosmetics, nail polish, makeup remover pads.

Dazzling Drawer Pulls

Update a plain dresser or night table by simply changing the knobs. Hardware stores and home centers have a wide variety and you can get ideas by wandering up and down the aisles. Sometimes creative solutions come from unexpected places.

Child's Night Table

For a night table in a child's room, try the unconventional. Rather than one center knob or drawer pull, use three. Round ceramic or plastic knobs come in primary colors such as red, green, blue, or yellow. Center one knob on the drawer front, then evenly space the other two on each side. If the dresser or night table has more than one drawer, mix the colors on each drawer. It's cute and practical.

Nautical Touch

For an older child's furniture, use rope rather than knobs for the drawer pulls. Turn regular cotton or nylon clothesline nautical blue by dipping it into fabric dye. Cut two 18-inch lengths and follow the directions on the bottle for dying. Let dry. Then attach two ½-inch screw eyes approximately 5 inches apart on the center of each drawer. Thread the rope through each and tie a knot to secure. For an alternative nautical theme, substitute boat cleats for drawer pulls.

Big Is Better

Give a plain piece of furniture character instantly by using oversized knobs that look like doorknobs rather than small-size drawer pulls.

Fancy That

Paint large round wooden knobs in a checkerboard pattern. Paint each knob white, then draw crossed lines in the center of the knob and apply a color in alternating spaces. Polka dots are easy to create. Just paint the knob, then use a pointed artist's brush or a Q-tip to apply dots in a random freehand manner. They needn't be perfectly round.

Sponging

Sponge painting is an easy standby for almost any decorating project, including knobs. Plain wooden knobs are easy to sponge in seconds. If you have a ready-to-finish bureau, consider sponging the entire piece, drawer pulls and all.

Pretty, Prettier, Prettiest

A floral porcelain knob will make any drawer look delicate and pretty. Interesting lamp finials can be used as the main attraction on a small piece of furniture with narrow drawers.

Fast and Fashionable

Everyday inexpensive items can be used to make decorating accents that are better and cheaper than similar items sold in boutiques.

Fringed Throw Pillows

Use large, fringed napkins in solids or beautiful prints to make throw pillows. They can be backed with felt, suede cloth, or velvet.

Tapestry for Pennies

Ralph Lauren's tapestry placemats might seem expensive at around $20 each, since you'll need four or six. But if used to make a pillow, you'll only need one and the expense for this item won't seem so great. They have a backing, so just open one end, add stuffing, and restitch closed. A cinch!

From Rags to Riches

Use a small scatter rag rug to make a large bolster pillow. Loosely stuff and place across the back of your sofa or on a bed. Looks casual, soft, and comfy.

Pocket Pillow

Use the bottom half of a pretty apron to make the perfect pillow for holding glasses and a paperback book right at hand. Look for the cute aprons printed with a row of kittens or ducks. Cut off the bib part of the apron and use the bottom portion with the pockets for the front of the pillow.

Hanky Sachets

Stitch two delicate, lace-edged hankies together to make pillow sachets for the linen closet or to place in dresser drawers. Fill with potpourri. Put them in boxes of off-season clothes to keep them smelling sweet while not in use.

New Seat Cover

If you have a needlepoint or hooked rug that is partially destroyed, use the good portion to upholster the seat of a chair. The same goes for an unrepairable quilt.

No-Sew Valances

Use a lacy tablecloth to drape over a dowel curtain pole for a fresh and airy valance. No sewing needed! Or use linen napkins. Place each one diagonally over the pole so one point hangs down. Continue to place napkins, overlapping slightly, along the pole to the width of the window.

Subtle Texture

Add texture without curtains at the windows. Use ordinary white window shades and sponge paint with a pastel color to match the room. For a really subtle effect add just a drop of yellow or raw umber to white. Mix well and sponge onto a white shade.

Tied in Knots

Fat white boat mooring line is great for curtain tiebacks. Make a hefty knot at each side and keep in place on a cup hook at the edges of the window.

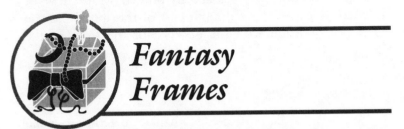

Fantasy Frames

Plain frames can be transformed with a faux finishing technique that is so easy to do (and the results are so great) that you'll want to do a whole bunch in different colors. The "fantasy finish" is created with two contrasting colors of glue paint made by mixing watercolor paint or food coloring with Elmer's glue. The techniques will work on any wood surface as well as on ceramic tile.

Mixing It Up

You'll need Elmer's Glue-All; small amounts of two different watercolor paints or food coloring; artist's brush; toothpick; clear spray varnish; fairly wide, flat wood frame.

Marbleizing

Mix together ¼ cup of glue and ¼ teaspoon of watercolor paint or food coloring. Brush the mixture onto the frame and spread it evenly over the surface. Wash the brush. Mix a contrasting color as you did the first and use the brush to drop a small pool of this glue paint onto the wet surface of the frame. Swirl it around with a toothpick to create a marble-like pattern. Set the frame aside to dry. It will take two days. When it is dry, spray a coat of varnish evenly over the frame. It will dry in minutes.

Mixing Colors

If you like the results of this technique, you might like to experiment with different colors. Food colorings are best for basic shades such as red, green, yellow, and blue. Watercolors come in a greater variety of colors and you can create soft pastels such as pale pink or gray, which resemble real marble. You can also create new patterns by sponging, swirling, feathering, or combing.

Sponging

Apply the first color mixture. Then, use a small piece of dry sponge to dab the second paint mixture over the surface at random.

Swirling

Use your fingers to create swirls in the mixture right on the frame. This is similar to finger painting. You can also use a piece of crumpled plastic wrap or newspaper for more interesting, textured swirls.

Feathering

Dip the point of a feather into the second mixture and stroke it lightly over the first color on the frame. Make crisscrosses and drag the feather tip to create interesting lines.

Combing

Drop the second color on one corner of the frame. Using a comb, drag the mixture down one side and then across the bottom. Turn the frame upside down and repeat.

Country Symbols

Certain design symbols have become synonymous with country style and we never seem to tire of them. The most popular are hearts, houses, doves, baskets, geese, and teddy bears. We see these designs used for stencils, on quilts, and in cross-stitch samplers. Add a little country warmth to your home by using country symbols to decorate a variety of accessories.

Sachets

Use scraps of red plaid, checked, or solid fabric to cut out heart-shaped appliqués to apply to 4-inch-square sachets made from contrasting fabric.

Kitchen Set

Decorate a pot holder with a heart appliqué, or add a row of hearts along the edge of linen dishtowels. Use a zigzag stitch on your machine or turn the raw edges under and hand stitch to the background fabrics.

Stencils

Stencil teddy bears around a child's room, along the front of the dresser, around a lamp shade, and on the back of a chair in the child's room for a happy, coordinated country look. If you can't find country stencils in your area, there are mail order sources. Call Stencil-Ease for a catalog. Their toll-free number is 1-800-334-1776.

Wallhanging

Make a quilted wallhanging using the schoolhouse pattern found in most quilting books. Or even easier, create a Log Cabin design from strips of fabric scraps.

Framed Stitches

Use scraps of fabric such as calicos, homespun, ticking, or solids to piece together a patchwork appliqué such as an apple, heart, or teddy bear and stitch it to a piece of background fabric. Then mat in an interesting wood frame.

Rows of Hearts

Cut six small hearts from different fabric scraps. Arrange and stitch them in three rows of two hearts each on a muslin background for framing.

Symbol of Welcome

The pineapple has always been a traditional symbol of welcome and hospitality. Use it to stencil a wooden plaque for your hallway. Add your family name in stencil letters on the wood beneath the pineapple.

Fun Furniture

You can get real bargains on ready-to-finish furniture that's perfect for country decorating. Paint or stain a blanket chest for a bedroom or to place in the hallway to hold boots and winter gear. Add a stenciled flock of geese or a vine of country flowers across the front. Or—need I say it again?—hearts!

Old-Fashioned Sampler

Early American samplers date back to colonial days. Cross-stitch embroidery was used to create neat, geometric rows that formed patterns, borders, numbers, letters, and scenes. The most popular motifs are adapted from American folk art, and you'll find a variety of kits with designs and all the materials at a craft shop or from a mail order source such as The Stitchery, 120 N. Meadows Rd., Medfield, MA 02052. Send $2 for their catalog.

Flower
Power

Creative Ways with Flowers

Decorating with garden flowers makes every room seem fresh and alive. Collect all sorts of containers for flowers and small plants, then match them up accordingly.

Pitchers

Fill a large white pitcher with a mixed arrangement of cut flowers, or with sprigs of tall green branches for a casual arrangement.

Goblets

Oversized glass goblets are perfect for short-stemmed flowers. Arrange several in the center of a dining table and intersperse candles between the goblets. The clear glass will reveal the green flower stems.

Plain and Simple

Place a spiked stem holder or small dish filled with marbles in the center of a large serving or mixing bowl and arrange just three or four long-stemmed delicate flowers, such as freesia, in the center so the stems meet at the base and fan out gracefully. This is especially nice on a sideboard or in the center of a long dining table.

Floral Hatbox

Use a pretty hatbox to hold small plants such as African violets or primroses. Line the hatbox with plastic. If the hatbox is too deep for the plants, turn a small bowl or dish upside down under the plants to raise them. Fill the area around the plants with Spanish moss.

Kitchen Color

Fill a long bread basket with pots of herbs and place it on the windowsill for ready access in cooking. Or use long, green metal window boxes. For interest, use large stencil letters and white acrylic paint to decorate with the name of the herbs across the bottom edge of the planter.

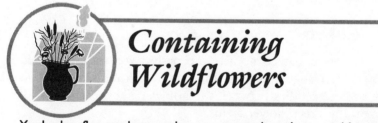

Containing Wildflowers

Yard sales, flea markets, and your own cupboards can yield interesting containers for flower arrangements and often suggest what should be put in them. For example, I have a sweet little white pitcher covered with tiny blue flowers and green leaves. The lip is chipped, so I don't use it for the table, but it's perfect for holding chicory with a few sprigs of mint.

Country Crock

Fill with a loose arrangement of Queen Anne's lace and blades of grass.

Terra-Cotta

A plain clay pot has a rustic quality. Use it to hold an arrangement of bright yellow cat's ear, field thistle, and fall astors.

Basket of Field Grass

Place a stem holder in the bottom of a deep bowl and set this into a country basket. Arrange with long blades of swamp grass and wheat-like stalks.

Travel Souvenir

I especially like to take home a flower as a reminder of a trip. One spring when my husband and I were in the south of France I picked bright orange poppies in a field and pressed them in my travel diary. Every time I read through the book I come across the pressed flowers. They remind me of that particular day.

While standing on the grass at my daughter's graduation I noticed little white flowers growing all around and picked a few. I pressed them in the photo album along with the pictures we took. They add to the pleasures of reliving that special day.

Beware!

Before picking wildflowers, please be advised there are endangered species that are here for everyone's enjoyment, but not for picking. When in doubt, do not pick.

Faking It!

New advances in the manufacture of silk flowers make them look so real you'll be tempted to water them. And you can't even tell an artificial tree after touching it, the barks and branches are so realistic.

Tips for Keeping Artificial Flowers Fresh for Years

1. Put polyester flowers in a solution of mild soap and lukewarm water. Rinse in clear water and hang upside down to air dry.
2. Wash the flowers twice a year.
3. Blow dust off with a hair dryer set on cool at a low speed.
4. Lightly dust with a feather duster.
5. Never dunk a hand-wrapped flower in water. It will ruin the tape's elasticity.
6. Dust large fake trees with a vacuum cleaner hose attached to the out-air hole.
7. Remove grease and grime by shaking flowers in a small bag containing half a cup of table salt. Insert just the heads of the flower and shake for two minutes. Remove any excess salt with a hair dryer.
8. Store loose artificial flowers in their original boxes.
9. When you put the arrangement away, put it in a large plastic bag and store in a cool, dry, dark place.

Potpourri from Your Garden

The use of potpourri for scenting homes goes way back. Not only was it used for driving away unpleasant odors when ventilation and sanitation were poor and houses damp, but it was used for curing ailments. In England, the floors of public meeting places such as churches were often strewn with sweet-smelling herbs such as mints, lavender, thyme, tansy, rosemary, and sage. It seems only natural that this early practice would lead to the making of fragrant bowls for scenting rooms.

Plants for Potpourri

Almost every garden contains a few plants that will yield suitable material for potpourri. Roses, lavender, carnations, sweet pea, geraniums, and violets as well as herbs are the mainstay of a good potpourri mixture. The addition of spices, such as cloves, cinnamon, allspice, and nutmeg, increases the potpourri possibilities.

Sweet Scents for the Bathroom

Fill a shallow basket, a ceramic jar, or a clear glass bowl with a potpourri mixture. This keeps a bathroom smelling fresh and looks especially pretty. I like to keep a bowl of potpourri in the linen closet. Every time I open the door I get a whiff of this lovely fresh scent and the linens all have a hint of scent.

Vacation Home

If you're in a rented house that doesn't smell quite like your own, add containers of potpourri here and there to create your own scent. It's like personal perfume.

Making Your Own Potpourri

There are two methods for making potpourri. The dry method entails completely drying all ingredients and will keep the color best. The moist method is often used when adding roses. This method preserves the scent best but discolors the petals. Store this potpourri in an opaque container.

Dry Method

Collect flowers just after they've opened when the dew has lifted. Spread them on a tray and place in a warm, shady, dry area where there is air circulation. It takes a day or two for the petals to become dry and crisp. Then mix them with a fixative such as orris root (some drugstores have this) and place in an airtight jar. Use about 1 ounce orris root to 2 pints dried petals. If you throw in a small package of Silica Gel (from a florist) it will ensure complete dryness. Leave for two or three days.

Moist Method

Gather petals and spread until they are partially dry, not crisp and dried out as above. It takes about twenty-four hours. Put a half-inch layer of petals in a jar, then sprinkle over with a little sea salt and repeat until the jar is about two-thirds full. Allow 1 cup of salt to 2 cups of petals. The jar can be filled over a period of a few days, but stir the contents before adding fresh layers. Keep the jar tightly closed and in a dark place for about ten days. Take out the mass of dried petals, separate, and toss, like making a salad. Place in an attractive container.

Pomander Balls

Create a fresh, citrus-scented pomander ball. Traditionally oranges are used for this, but I like to use lemons and limes in the summer. Simply pierce the fruit with evenly spaced, crisscrossing lines of cloves or start at one end and make a spiral. This will be easier if you first puncture the holes with a knitting needle. As the fruit dries, the spaces between the cloves will close up. Sprinkle the fruit with a little nutmeg or cinnamon to add to the perfume. Arrange the fruit in a wooden or white ceramic bowl for a summery, fresh table decoration. They even look good in a colander on the kitchen counter and will give off a wonderful scent. If you tie a ribbon around each one and hang them in the closets they will keep your clothes smelling fresh.

Porcelain Flowers

You can spray paint plastic flowers from the five-and-ten-cent store and they will look as though they were made of porcelain. There's a wide variety of ways to use them for decorating plain objects. The variations you can create are only as limited as the flowers that are available. Flowers of any type, color, or size can be used, but the smaller blossoms look best.

Preparation

Select a group of flowers for a bouquet. Flowers that come as a cluster or have many blossoms on one stalk can be cut apart to create a fuller arrangement. Use leaves and stems as well. Insert the individual flowers in a foam block (available at a florist's shop) and spray with white paint. Keep moving the can back and forth as you spray so you won't overload one area. You may have to approach the flowers from above, under, and inside in order to coat them thoroughly. None of the original color should show. Let them dry.

Making an Arrangement

Remove the flowers and arrange in a selected container. You might choose a pretty teacup with a delicate design, baskets in all sizes and shapes, a bowl, tin mugs, or a pitcher. The baskets can also be spray painted. Place a piece of florist's foam into the container and insert the flowers one at a time as you create the arrangement.

Decorate a Frame

Decorate a frame to display a wedding picture. Spray paint a dime-store frame. Determine where the flowers will go. You can either surround the entire frame or create a small sprig of buds and leaves around two opposite corners. Using white glue, dab dots where the flowers will be placed. Lay each flower in position and leave it to dry before inserting your picture.

Party Flowers

For a special occasion, dress up the punch bowl with flower-embedded ice cubes. Float the pretty ice cubes in drinks, or pile them around a glass serving dish filled with ice cream.

Frozen Flowers

To make floral ice cubes, put a tiny flower or petal in each section of an ice tray. Fill halfway with water and freeze solid. Then, fill to the top with water and freeze again. When you freeze in two stages, the flowers end up in the middle of the ice, rather than floating to the top.

Table Decoration

For a quick and easy table decoration fill a shallow glass container halfway with water. Float small, round candles, designed to be placed in water, and drop small flower heads or petals among them. If you place the dish on a table in front of a mirror you will create maximum sparkle.

Tapers

Secure tall thin candles with florist's putty in a shallow dish of water. Float mint sprigs with red and white baby carnation heads or other small flowers for an instant centerpiece.

Pretty Planters

Good-looking planters don't have to be expensive. In fact, you can be creative with ordinary household objects.

Salad Bowl

A round, wooden salad bowl is perfect for a country bouquet. Use a Styrofoam block available in garden shops and place it in the center of the bowl. Cut and insert flower stems to create a rounded arrangement to conform to the shape of the bowl. Fill with water.

Bag It!

A brown paper bag and iridescent paint can be used to create an unusual holder for a bunch of roses and Queen Anne's lace. The paint comes in squirt tubes. Swirl the paint over the bag in a random pattern, then wad a paper towel and dab the paint to create a sponged effect. Allow some unpainted sections to show through. Let dry.

Arrange flowers in a glass or wide-mouthed jar and insert into the bag. Turn the top of the bag down two or three times to make a finished edge, gather the bag under the turned edge, and wrap with a cord, ribbon, or natural vine.

Paper Bucket

One of the most versatile items is a paper paint bucket available in most hardware or paint stores. They cost about fifty cents and can be covered with spray paint, wallpaper, Con-Tact paper, or wrapping paper. You can decorate them with a stencil design, decoupage, or embroidered ribbon. For an elegant container, cover the bucket with marbled paper found in an art store. This is a pretty way to take a plant to a friend in the hospital or as a housewarming gift or to brighten up a dull corner or table in your own home.

Pressing Events

Pressing flowers is an enjoyable way to preserve your garden bouquet. Pressed flowers can be used for all sorts of decorating projects.

Flowers That Press Best

Naturally flat flowers such as pansies provide the best results, but it's not necessary to limit yourself to these. Flowers that press well include the black-eyed Susan, cosmos, lavender, Queen Anne's lace, tansy, and zinnia.

Colors

The color retention is best in yellow flowers such as buttercups and daisies. Orange flowers also retain their color well and green stays bright. Red and purple often turn brown. When choosing flowers to be pressed, add leaves, stems, and blades of grass as well.

Pressing Process

You'll need several pieces of white blotter paper or sheets of paper toweling, pieces of corrugated paper (a cut-up paper box will do) the same size as the blotter paper, several heavy books, and a variety of fresh flowers.

Place several flowers and leaves on a piece of the blotting paper so they don't overlap. Each sheet can be filled with as many flowers as can comfortably fit. Cover the flowers with another piece of blotting paper and over this place a corrugated board. Repeat this procedure until you have a stack of four to six layers. Pile several heavy books on top and leave undisturbed for a minimum of one week. The blotting paper will absorb the moisture in the flowers as they dry out.

Handle with Care

Once the flowers are dry they should be handled carefully. Use a pair of tweezers to lift the flowers from the blotter paper and arrange them on a fabric or paper background. Rearrange them until you're satisfied.

Arrangements Under Glass

Create an arrangement under glass on a coffee table, or on a serving tray. A glass shop or hardware store will cut the glass to size. A lace handkerchief or pastel calico fabric makes a beautiful background for a flower design. Or use pastel paper against which you can arrange pressed violets, buttercups, rose petals, or delicate ferns. Illustrations made of pressed flowers can be matted and framed for an interesting and inexpensive project. Blades of grass are useful when creating an illustration. Place them between flowers as delicate filler. For a finishing touch, glue a border of grosgrain ribbon around the illustration. Lay the piece of glass carefully on top of the entire scene, ribbon and all.

Greeting Cards

Make individualized greeting cards with pressed flowers. Buy blank cards with envelopes in an art supply or stationery store. Arrange a few flowers on the front of the card, then secure them in place by covering with a piece of clear Con-Tact paper. Cut the self-adhesive paper slightly larger than your card, press over the flowers, and smooth down with your hand. Then trim the excess around the edges. This technique can be used to decorate placecards for a party.

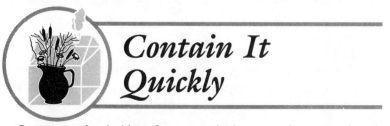

Contain It Quickly

Containers for holding flowers and plants can be created with things you have right in your own home. No need to buy expensive vases or cachepots.

Turn the Knob

Turn unusual doorknobs upside down for bud vases. Group them on a table or line them on a windowsill. Fill with tiny buds. Use one on a bathroom shelf.

A Great Scoop

Wooden grain scoops are often found in antique shops. They come in a variety of sizes. Use one to hold a potted plant or dried country arrangement.

Clearly Stated

A glass apothecary jar is just the thing for a kitchen bouquet. Use one or group several.

Leave It Be

Wrap galax leaves around a small vase or jar and secure with a pin.

Cream of the Crop

Use novelty creamers for small bouquets. Group them together or place one in front of each person's place at the table.

Gift Boxes

For a dinner party, group graduated sizes of shiny colored gift boxes. Stuff with tissue, then add a small jar in the center of each to hold a bouquet. Tie a ribbon around each box.

Scented

Use empty perfume bottles to hold small buds on a dressing table or windowsill.

Twiggy

Surround a planter with sticks or twigs standing on end and tie with natural-colored twine, jute, or rope.

Fabric Elegance

Place a plant in the center of a square of elegant fabric, such as moiré or tapestry, bring up the edges, and gather the fabric around the plant. It should extend slightly above the rim of the pot. Tie with a satin or grosgrain ribbon.

Cinnamon Sense

Surround a plant with cinnamon sticks placed upright and secure with a red ribbon.

 *Arrangements with Flowers, Vegetables, and Fruit*

There are many ways to dress up any area of your home with an arrangement of flowers. They can be as casual or elaborate as you feel inspired to make them. A friend of mine is an artist who creates unconventional arrangements by combining vegetables and fruit with flowers. His suggestions will surely have you looking at your garden and the produce department of the supermarket with an entirely new eye.

Daffodils and Squash

Start an arrangement with a plastic, tin, or metal container surrounded by moss and secured with twisted raffia tied in a knot. Fill with water and place a piece of chicken wire or mesh across the top. This will hold the stems. Use a variety of daffodils, cut very short, to make a rounded, tightly knit group just above the rim of the container. Wire summer squash and insert them here and there in the arrangement. Do the same with long, skinny green and yellow peppers to add a bit of height; add a bright orange pepper, lemons, fat, white mushrooms, and a yellow apple or pear. It's a delightful study of shapes and shades of color.

Broccoli and Cauliflower

Combine small bunches of flowers with florettes of broccoli and cauliflower. Insert a Styrofoam block into a basket to hold the stems. Keep the flowers low and tightly grouped.

Citrus and Tomatoes

Drop a few lemons and a lime in the bottom of a tall glass vase. Then insert long-stemmed flowers such as California poppies or long branches of yellow forsythia. For red flowers, place a few cherry tomatoes in the bottom of the glass container. They will add an element of surprise as well as color. Drop peaches or an orange in a glass vase that holds orange tiger lilies.

Creative Containers

As for containers, anything goes: a metal watering can, an egg cup for tiny buds, a scooped-out red pepper to hold branches of berries, a wire basket filled with moss, a silver chalice, or a wooden salad bowl. Surround a container with stalks of wheat held in place with a ribbon or raffia.

Green and Purple

For a green arrangement, add avocado and eggplant combined with green and purple flowers. Surround bunches of violets with lettuce and cabbage leaves and add sprigs of different varieties of parsley for a tightly packed arrangement.

Grapes and Roses

Use bunches of grapes as the basis for a creation that includes tiny roses and thistle, or grape hyacinth. Insert a few stems of grapes in a vase with peonies.

Onions and Pine Boughs

Arrange a bowl of red onions, pomegranate, and apples and insert branches of evergreens.

Natural Does It

Surround a natural-colored bouquet with small pebbles and white shells or create a dish garden with small stones. Insert tiny buds and pieces of moss here and there. Place one perfect gardenia inside a conch shell.

Hats Off to You!

Turn a straw hat upside down and place a glass inside to hold anemones or white tulips.

Art from an Artichoke

Use a full artichoke as a flower holder. Cut a hole in the top and insert one beautiful freesia or a bunch of lily-of-the-valley. Fill a pretty ceramic mixing bowl with a bunch of broccoli, parsley, small artichokes, and hydrangeas.

Oranges and Tangerines

Create a base of oranges and tangerines, then add orange and yellow tulips, yellow roses, and green leaves.

Dried Alternatives

Consider prunes, raisins, dates, and nuts to use with wheat stalks and straw flowers.

Summer's Ripeness

Use ripe peaches, plums, and cherries to spice up any floral arrangement. Or use them as the starting point on which a creative bouquet is built. Pile them on a plate or in a bowl and insert stems of flowers in colors that go best with them.

Less Formal

For a full and colorful arrangement of zinnias, coreopsis, and chrysanthemums or any stiff, formal flowers, add vines of ivy to trail from the container. This will give it a more uninhibited feeling.

Collections

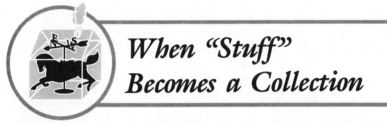

When "Stuff" Becomes a Collection

We're comfortable surrounded by familiar and well-loved things. But most of us have too much "stuff." Creative people know how to arrange their things better than others, and then their "stuff" is called a collection.

What Is a Collection?

A group of similar things artfully arranged is usually referred to as a collection. A collection doesn't have to be of any monetary value and there is no specific criteria for collecting something.

Many collections started by accident. Perhaps you bought a Toby mug at a flea market, then another at a yard sale, and now you find yourself looking for Toby mugs whenever you're traveling. A collection can start with anything that attracts your interest for whatever reason.

A collection is usually not purchased as a whole, but rather is collected piece by piece. That's the fun of a collection.

First you have the experience of finding a new piece and then you have the experience of seeing it displayed with the rest of the collection. There is no end to the number you can add. Each piece is a reminder of a different time or place where the item was purchased.

Personalized Collection

A collection is an individual and personal statement. Sometimes a collection is visited upon the unsuspecting. My husband's uncle had the misfortune of being nicknamed "Bunny." Need I say more? Everyone knew exactly what to give him for Christmas and birthdays. He had glass bunnies, ceramic bunnies, stuffed bunnies, large and miniature bunnies. And because they were gifts he could never give any of them away.

Collections I Have Known

1. Oversized crocks filling a niche of shelves.
2. Antique mechanical toys displayed on narrow shelves.
3. Black and white photographs of family members lining a narrow wall area and all framed alike with narrow black frames.
4. Teddy bears playfully arranged around a room as if they were perfectly at home. One sits in a child's high chair, one is propped in a bookshelf, another is tucked into the arm of a sofa.
5. Small wooden boxes of all sorts with interesting fittings and handles. Some are grouped, others stacked, larger ones on the floor—all are used to hold something so they are useful as well as decorative.
6. Baskets hanging from a rafter or beam, or lined

up on a bench or shelf always within easy access for practical uses.

7. Glass lamps or pretty vases grouped on top of a highboy or sideboard in a dining room near a window to catch the light.

8. Quilts on beds, as wallhangings, as tablecloths, over a sofa or chair. Damaged quilts can be cut up and used to cover pillows.

9. Early samplers simply framed and grouped on one wall or over a fireplace.

10. Early American tools mounted and carefully arranged on a wall or set on a table to be admired and handled.

11. Carefully arranged books filling an entire wall as the focal point of an otherwise stark and uncluttered room. Great for the soul!

12. Unusual antique eyeglass cases laid out on a table with a few carefully selected complementary objects.

Affordable Americana

There is a growing awareness and appreciation in this country for things that are handmade and have historic value. If you're thinking about purchasing one item for your home this year, American folk art is affordable and is appreciating in value.

Beginning a Collection

A room needn't be cluttered with objects to be aesthetically pleasing or comfortable. It's smart to collect one good piece at a time rather than amassing lots of possessions. If you have young children, furnish with the fewest necessities. Life will be infinitely easier. Rooms that are left quite bare can be attractive if each piece is carefully chosen. This is practical but enables you to select and add one piece at a time as is affordable.

What to Buy

Advice from a dealer to a new collector: "Buy something that speaks to you. If it makes you happy to look at it, don't think about its future commercial value. It will always be valuable to you."

Quilts

Quilts have taken an important place in decorating with folk art and are the best buy around. Aside from use as a bedcovering, a quilt is an inexpensive way to have "art" on the walls. You can always find an affordable antique quilt in your color scheme and a design to go with your style. While most quilt patterns are country style, bold, two-color, geometric patterns look surprisingly contemporary.

Hooked Rugs

Finally old enough to be considered valuable, American hooked rugs with floral and geometric patterns, primitive animal motifs, and charming sayings have become as popular as quilts. It's always easy to find a place for these charming accessories.

Painted Furniture

Furniture pieces from the eighteenth and early nineteenth centuries are interesting and add personality to any room.

They reside happily side by side with quilts and other collectables.

Decoys

Colorful wooden duck and fish decoys are easy to find. They are both decorative and usable. Group them on a table rather than having them spread about. This will create more impact.

Memory Art

Samples of memory art, which is made of bits of broken glass and chinaware embedded in such objects as umbrella stands and boxes, are fun to collect and display.

Moveable Art

Weathervanes and whirligigs have always been a symbol of American folk art. There is an endless variety of styles, some more interesting and valuable than others. Don't be put off by the crudeness of craftsmanship. This is what makes them so charming. Place one by a window to catch the breezes. Mechanical toys also add playfulness to any area.

Bits of Romance

Vintage lace will always add a touch of elegance on a table or bed. It's the simplest way to make a room fresh and airy for summer.

Hobo No More

"Tramp art" is usually found in the form of boxes made from pieces of whittled wood of varied sizes and shapes. Its humble beginnings are evident in the finished results and the objects are highly regarded by many collectors of American folk art.

Outside Art

Canes and walking sticks with carved handles are cropping up here and there, and the marvelously playful carved walking sticks from Kentucky artists will be valuable collectables in the near future. These artists, called "outsiders" because they are not of the mainstream, are being discovered by gallery owners all over the country. For now, this primitive artwork is still affordable.

Baskets

Baskets are appreciated as a mainstay for quick home decorating. However, the most interesting are old and darkened Nantucket lightship baskets with ivory turnings and American Indian baskets. Indian artifacts of all sorts are prized collectables.

Frame Favorite Collectables

Nothing adds interest to a room more quickly and easily than custom-framed photos, artwork, and memorabilia. The first step to successful decorating with picture frames is to select creative and interesting artwork or items for framing. Aside from photographs, posters, and paintings, consider the following:

A Family Heirloom

This might be a piece of needlepoint or tapestry, or a family tree.

A Mom's Treasure

The first birthday card your child ever sent to you is something worth preserving. Treat it like a masterpiece. What better way than matting and hanging it in a colorful frame?

Pure Poetry

Framing a favorite poem or illustration from a book is an inexpensive way to decorate with something that pleases you.

Personally Yours

Frame a diary entry from a special day. It will have meaning every time you see it framed and hanging in a special niche.

Quilts and Wallhangings

Add country warmth and charm with a quilted item of any size on the wall. Do not hang where the sun will fade the fabric.

Say It with Love

A stenciled or cross-stitched saying adds a personal touch to the kitchen.

Ask the Pros

Framing materials come in numerous colors, styles, and textures. Professional picture framers can provide you with a wide selection of moldings and mats that are appropriate for the items to be framed.

Getting the Hang of It

When hanging a single piece of art, always hang it at eye level. Placing a piece too high or low is distracting and draws attention away from it.

Balancing Act

Try to achieve balance when positioning framed work on a wall. For example, if the picture will hang over furniture, center it above the piece, or line it up with one edge of the furniture. Generally, a large frame doesn't look too great above a small piece of furniture.

Drawing Attention

A dark frame on a light wall will attract the most attention.

Busy Background

Don't hesitate to hang pictures on patterned wallpaper. Busy walls, however, need bold, strong frames and artwork.

Liven Things Up

A plain room can come alive with an arrangement of artwork on one wall. Consider mixing shapes such as ovals, squares, and rectangles in one group.

Small Room

If your room is small with low ceilings, stay away from group displays. Hanging pictures close together will make the room seem crowded and smaller.

Fool the Eye

If you don't have a headboard, hang a large framed picture above the bed to add interest.

Conservation Know-how

Frame your work with conservation in mind. Years of exposure can cause fading, especially to fabric such as a quilt. Consult a professional or do research before framing.

Family Fun

Groups of vacation snapshots can create a wall of interest in a hallway and will become a conversation piece. This is always fun to share.

Appropriate Framing

If you have something sentimental, such as an old valentine, a piece of lace, a pressed flower corsage, or a wedding invitation, an ornate frame will add a romantic touch.

Seashell Inspirations

A walk on the beach can't help but inspire us to collect shells. This humble collection is a nice reminder of a vacation, but what to do with them isn't always immediately apparent. The good news is their natural colors fit into any decorating scheme and the variety of shapes makes for naturally interesting displays.

A Simple Display

Often, the simplest idea is the nicest. Fill a glass jar with your collection of shells and set it in front of a window. The light will reflect on them and create a delightful display. Or pile the shells into an interesting basket and set it on a side table. They are always tempting to touch.

Shell Collage

The most ordinary shells can look beautiful when arranged in a collage. Glue them in symmetrical rows on a piece of weathered wood and hang in a hallway or bathroom.

Chiming In

Wind chimes made from shells are a delight to the senses. Each type of shell has its own sound depending on size and shape. Wind chimes are easy to make because most shells have a hole through which you can string nylon; then simply tie each shell to a piece of wood.

Type Cast

Sea glass, stones, and dried, whitened bones are interesting when arranged in a type drawer. This is a flat wooden tray divided into small partitions that once held printer's type. These trays can be found at flea markets, second-hand shops, and through mail order sources. To create a display, glue a found object into each section of the type drawer and hang it on the wall as if it were a framed picture.

Shell Flowers

You can make flowers from small seashells. Using tweezers and glue, arrange shell "petals" on an object such as the top of a box or basket. This is a nice way to decorate a mirror frame in a bathroom.

To make a shell flower picture, use seaweed and sea grasses for your flower stems and compose a picture on heavy colored paper. Add a frame and hang with picture wire.

Family Memories

Preserve family memories, special invitations, photographs, newspaper clippings, and important announcements in a decorative way.

Family Memory Board

This is an elegant alternative to a bulletin board or magnets on the fridge. Begin with a 2 x 3-foot bulletin board, stapler, thumbtacks, 8–10 yards of 1-inch-wide grosgrain ribbon, and a yard of pretty fabric. (It can match something in the room. Belgian linen or moiré is nice. Don't use stripes or plaids.)

Center the bulletin board face down on the wrong side of the fabric. Trim the fabric so you have 2–3 inches extra on all sides. Wrap it tautly and staple to the back of the board. Working from the center outward, cut and arrange strips of ribbon in a symmetrical, crisscrossing pattern of a grid or diamonds with 2–3-inch spaces between. Cut the ribbons so you have enough extra at each end to wrap around and staple to the back of the bulletin board. When you have something to remember, jot it on a pretty piece of paper and tuck it into a ribbon "holder" along with invitations, snapshots, theater tickets, etc.

Personal Travelogue

It's fun to arrange photos of a recent trip, which might normally go into a scrapbook, in a collage on the top of an occasional round table covered with fabric. A piece of glass cut to size holds everything in place and you can change the whole thing next year.

Wedding Collage

Combine momentos with photographs. For a romantic, old-fashioned theme, arrange wedding snapshots with bits of lace and ribbon and pressed flowers overlapping the edges here and there.

A Very Good Year

For an anniversary or birthday gift, combine personal photographs from a specific year with cutout magazine images or sayings, a political promotion, an announcement of an event from the paper, a school pendant—any period piece from that year. Arrange them on a piece of heavy paper and frame.

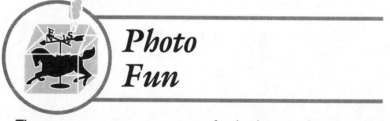

Photo Fun

There are many ways to preserve family photographs other than placing them in an album or simply framing them. A new baby creates a flurry of picture taking. Select a series of these shots taken during a child's first year, or photographs taken of your children at special events or milestones in their lives. These can be used to create great grandparent gifts.

Photo Placemats

These make the perfect gift for grandparents and are fun for family get-togethers. You'll need a selection of snapshots, plastic placemats, mounting adhesive (available in art stores), and clear plastic Con-Tact paper.

Assemble and trim a group of photos so you have a variety of shapes. Using the mounting adhesive, make an arrangement of the photos on the front of each placemat. To protect the photos cover with clear adhesive paper.

Framing Baby

Mount a baby's picture on a painted, wooden plaque. Then glue a ½-inch-wide ribbon around the picture's edge. Or surround the picture with rows of baby beads.

Bridal Best

For a wedding picture, cut out the center of a doily and mount it over the photo so that the bride is surrounded by a lacy border. Set in a frame.

Notable Notions

Rickrack, dried flowers, lace, and decorative ribbons can all be used to offset the edges of a photograph before mounting and framing.

Desk Accessories

For a personal touch on your desk, glue favorite photos to the tops of small containers. Aspirin tins, film cartons, and plastic pillboxes can hold paper clips and stamps.

File It!

Paint a recipe file box and mount a photo, cut to size, on the top. Use this to organize your photographs. If you enjoy taking nature photos, choose the best one to place on the top of the box and file the others under appropriate headings for easy retrieval.

Changing Scene

Have a glass top cut for a coffee table and use this area for an ever-changing photo gallery. Family and friends will enjoy the conversation piece.

Vacation Photos

Many of your best photographs can be made into distinctive and personal gifts for holiday giving or for decorating your home. This is a good way to bring your vacation experience home with you to enjoy year-round.

Preserving a Day at the Beach

If you plan a trip to the beach, collect a variety of shells to be used for framing the pictures you take while there. Center and mount your vacation photo on a piece of heavy cardboard that's 1 inch larger all around than the photograph. Arrange the seashells around the border, allowing some of the shells to overlap the edges of the picture. Use Elmer's white glue or a hot glue gun (sold in five-and-ten or craft stores) to apply each shell. Overlap them so they are clustered to create a nice frame. Let dry thoroughly, then attach a tab to the back for hanging.

Colorful Photos

Plan to photograph your children dressed in their most colorful T-shirts. Then use colored pencils to make a frame for the picture. Use a craft knife to cut the pencils to the size of each side of the photograph. Arrange two or three pencils around the picture and hold in place temporarily with tape. Buy a mat to fit the exact size of the outside dimension around the "pencil frame." Reposition the pencils around the mat background and glue each one in place. Let dry before placing the whole thing over the photograph. Use masking tape to attach the picture to the back of the framed mat, then attach a hanging tab to the back as well.

Map It Out

If you will be vacationing at a historic or landmark area, plan to take photographs of the family at different recognizable spots. Then be sure to save a map of the town. When your pictures are developed you can combine the two for a memorable keepsake. This is a project the whole family will enjoy.

Match the photos to the areas in which the pictures were taken. Crop each photograph so it fits on various sections of the map. Glue in position. When all the photos are in place, frame and hang in an area where your vacation can be relived again and again.

Nature Scene

Take a series of photographs of flowers or natural vegetation indigenous to the area. Or find houses with beautiful plantings in window boxes or small gardens and mount the best photograph on top of a pretty box to hold the other pictures.

Theme Photos

Pick a theme, such as historic houses or landmark areas, and create a series that can be enlarged for framing. If you've taken slides, have color photocopy enlargements made from these for an interesting and different approach to framed photos. This can be done at your local copy center. You'll be surprised at how good these copies can be. If there's a local art gallery in the vacation area, stop by for some inspirational ideas.

Personal Treasures

Even the most mundane items, if artfully arranged, can be used to create an interesting assemblage for display. We all collect something that is valuable only to us. While stuck away in a drawer it's just an accumulation, but made into an arrangement it can become dramatic and interesting.

Preserving Love Letters

Precious letters can be displayed in a discreet way for personal enjoyment. Arrange them in a collage fashion on the inside of a bathroom or closet door or on top of a dresser or trunk, and glue them to the surface. Add a coat of varnish, polyurethane, or shellac to preserve and protect them. Test the chemical over the ink on one letter to be sure it won't bleed before selecting the right coating.

Art in a Drawer

Create a diorama from childhood memories. Typical ingredients might be ordinary things from your past, such as pieces of plastic doll furniture, a jewelry box with the dancing ballerina missing, a set of jacks, an assortment of Crackerjack prizes, a half-finished embroidered lace handkerchief, a faded piece of patchwork, and an assortment of buttons. Use these items to create a display. The collection can be made up of anything that holds memories for you.

Finishing Touches Make Craftwork More Professional

Professional craftspeople know the importance of paying meticulous attention to the finishing details. A beautiful painting can be ruined if the framing is sloppy. The same is true of a cross-stitch sampler or needlepoint scene. Here are some tips for making your handcrafts look more professional.

Material

Always use the best materials you can find for your craft. Since you're committing many hours of your time, the end result should look as good as possible. A synthetic yarn may be more practical than wool, silk, or cotton, but let's face it, nothing looks better than the real thing.

Blocking Needlework

Needlepoint and cross-stitch gets distorted and out of shape while you're working on it either by hand or in a frame.

Whether made into a pillow or meant for framing, the finished work should be steamed and blocked, if possible by a professional. Take it to a local needlework shop or look in the Yellow Pages for this service.

Little Things Mean a Lot

If your needlework is made into a pillow, the backing fabric, trim, stuffing, and stitching should be worthy of the artwork. This may be costly, but it surely is worthwhile in the long run. If you can't spend the money to have it done professionally, take the time to learn how to do this properly and buy the best material you can afford. For example, a velvet backing is much nicer than a leftover piece of calico and will change the entire appearance of your pillow. Check out trimmings, tassels, cording, and ribbons. These will definitely add that professional touch and increase the value of your piece if you intend to sell your work. For more ideas, look at high-priced boutique items to see how they are finished.

Matting and Framing

Professional matting and framing will give you decorating options so your craftwork will be an interesting accessory in your home. It will do much to elevate it to the status of art.

Fabulous Furniture

If you do furniture finishing, choose pieces that are worthy of the technique you use. Even in the world of unfinished furniture there are well-designed pieces and those that are poorly crafted. Starting with a good piece will enhance your work.

Wallhangings

A quilted wallhanging should be carefully pressed so all sides are perfectly even. There are many ways to hang a quilt. Choose the best way for your project; consider the area where it will hang and the most appropriate method for its size and follow the directions to a T. Take the time to research products such as frames and stretchers made specifically for this purpose.

Placing It Right

If you make baskets, ceramics, and other three-dimensional objects, consider where and how they will be displayed. A nice setting for any handmade item will enhance its appreciation. Try placing it in different areas of the house. Set it apart on an interesting table and where the background doesn't fight for attention. Or arrange it with other items that are appropriate. In other words, take time to find the best way to show it off.

Using It Won't Abuse It

Crafts are more often made to be used than to be simply admired. By definition, crafts are "of the people" and were originally made to respond to a need. The more a handmade item is used, the more it is appreciated. It becomes part of one's life and thus enhances the quality of life. No craftwork should be so precious as to be untouchable.

Seasonal Changes

Spring Spruce-Ups

When spring arrives we all want to clean out the cobwebs, take down the heavy drapes, roll up the carpets, and lighten up every room in the house. It isn't necessary to redo everything at once. Small changes can make a big difference.

Fabrics

Nothing changes the look of a room as quickly and easily as fabric. For do-it-yourself home decorators, McCall's Pattern Company offers patterns for pillows; whimsical swags with rosettes; and bed, table, and chair coverings. Every spring the fabric houses bring out an entirely new line, so it's worth a trip to the fabric shop.

Window Treatments

Romantic swag valances replace heavy cornices. Sheers replace draperies.

Bedrooms

Bed treatments are taking a romantic turn with pillows piled on top of each other. There are ruffled shams and heart-shaped, round, and square pillows of all sizes adorned with ruffles, shirred corded edges, or tassels. All the pattern books now have extensive home decorating sections, so even the novice sewer can make lavish accessories inexpensively.

Cheer Up with Paint

Did you ever think of painting the inside of a closet pale yellow for a quick lift? The yellow interior will brighten the closet and your spirits. Reline closet shelves with a fresh springtime pattern. It's amazing how much mileage you'll get from this simple act.

Slip into Summer

Summertime usually dictates a more casual decorating style for easy and relaxed living. Parts of the country where it's warm most of the year often influence trends that are introduced to areas with only a short summer season. Here are some ideas for casual, summer decorating, culled from designer friends in various parts of the country.

From California

Slipcovers in heavy cotton, duck, or linen are best in white or beige. Set the table with textured damask tablecloths and napkins.

From a Southern Perspective

Big, tropical floral prints in faded colors are reminiscent of the 1920s or '30s. Use them on everything from sofas to tables.

From Designers Everywhere

White chinaware is still more attractive than any other as a background for serving a meal. Set the table with white tablecloths and lace-trimmed napkins (very large). This is a look that's always perfectly right for summer. Add one color, such as green or bright orange, in the center of the table.

The Greening of Summer

Large green placemats with white or green and white napkins are terrific on top of a pine table or outdoors on a white patio table, or on top of white linen. Green and white checked fabric is a change of pace from blue and white and still is a classic pattern. It's bold and bright for seat cushions and throw pillows on the patio or deck.

When Old Looks New

Big florals on a green and white striped background is an interesting look from a past decade. It resembles fabric used for housedresses in the '30s and '40s and seems antique and new at the same time.

Waterside

If you live by the beach or have a pool, cover outdoor cushions with bright-colored or brightly striped terry cloth towels. It's practical and pretty, even if only used temporarily.

Summer
Breezes

When the weather turns hot we tend to do less, which includes house care. There are lots of ways to simplify our homes for the lazy, hazy days of summer.

Airy Wicker

Wicker furniture, especially the all-weather pieces from Lloyd Flanders, is light and airy for use indoors and out. Even the fabric-covered cushions are weatherproof and dry out quickly after becoming wet. Replace an upholstered chair with a wicker one.

Furniture

Drape a side table with a cool colored sheet. If any of your furniture needs a new finish, consider pale blue or aqua paint.

White Is Cool

If a room needs repainting, nothing looks fresher than white. Put a drop of pink or yellow in the paint to take away the deadness of hospital white.

Floors

Remove room carpets and add scatter rugs, or use no rugs at all if you have nice wooden floors. Dhurries come in all sizes and cool pastel colors. They're practical and easy to care for. A sisal rug is natural in color and inexpensive.

Put Away Knickknacks

Remove knickknacks and replace them with one important piece, such as an American folk-art whirligig or a basket filled with flowers. And by the way, folk art and crafts are becoming the hottest collectables, so this might be a good time to start a collection. See pages 247–52 for suggestions.

Bare Your Windows

If you don't need to cover windows for privacy, removing curtains and draperies for summer creates instant light in the rooms. If you need some sort of covering, try sheers or a panel of lace. Or use shades that can be pulled down only when needed.

Outdoor Chairs

If you have those ubiquitous wire chairs on the patio, you know how uncomfortable they are. Try covering thin foam cushions with pillowcases for a pretty and comfortable look.

Dark Wood

If you have dark wooden pieces of furniture, add a lace-edged linen runner or table cover to lighten the top. Place a white bowl or glass vase of fresh wildflowers on top.

Fabric and Trims

To lighten upholstered furniture, add a couple of throw pillows covered with a summertime print. All-white textured pillows can be trimmed with piping to match the fabric on the sofa or chairs. Add a wide, striped ruffle to a floral chintz pillow. Cover fat cording with contrasting fabric to edge a tablecloth that drops to the floor.

Flowers

Place herbs in large clay pots on windowsills. Keep a glass vase filled with white flowers on the side table or in the middle of the dining table. Fill a white pitcher or bowl with a loose arrangement of wildflowers and herbs or mint, which will add a fresh aroma to the air.

Unusual Planters

Add a thin coating of whitewash to terra-cotta pots. Paint the pots white, then wipe away most of the paint, leaving a hint of white film to lighten the clay color.

Romantic Bathroom

Make your bathroom inviting. Spray paint a small wicker basket white. Add dabs of pink acrylic paint over the entire basket. Place a lacy doily in the basket and fill with potpourri. Tie a delicate embroidered ribbon to the handle.

Trim hand towels with lace, crocheted, or ribbon edgings. For a no-sew technique, use fusible webbing and press the trim onto the towel. It will stay through repeated washings.

On the Wall

Create a display of miniatures on a bathroom wall. Mat and frame botanical greeting cards, old family snapshots, or pressed flowers. Look for interesting frames at yard sales or in antique shops.

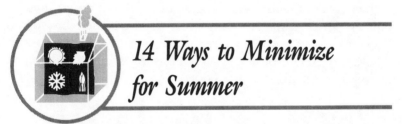

14 Ways to Minimize for Summer

For summer living, an uncluttered approach to decorating can be liberating. Cleansing a home is like going on a diet. Eliminate the fat and take stock. Here are fourteen tips for putting your house on a diet.

1. Do you really need a table piled with books that you've read or don't intend to read for a while?
2. You don't need a wool afghan over the sofa all summer. Have it cleaned and pack it away with mothballs until the weather gets cool again.

3. If the tabletops look bare, add only one thing. Just one.

4. Do you really need the canisters and all the small appliances on top of the kitchen counter?

5. What about the country accessories, such as baskets, and nonessentials that gather dust and no longer give you pleasure? Part with them until fall.

6. Organize the bathroom clutter into pretty containers and find out-of-the-way places for most of it. One basket on a shelf can hold everything within easy access.

7. Move your wall pictures around for a change of pace. Try exchanging a group of small pictures for one large one. It doesn't take much effort to create a new look in this way.

8. Move the furniture around for a different perspective. Do you always sit in the same seat at the dining table? Change seats to get another look at the room while you're eating. This will give you fresh ideas.

9. Buy an interesting trunk to use as an end or coffee table and for storing extra pillows, quilts, etc.

10. If removing things makes you uncomfortable, try exchanging. Move things from one room to another. Once it's out of its usual place it will look new.

11. Temporarily cover the throw pillows with light fabric or a textured white or natural linen.

12. Use white candlesticks and always white candles.

13. Arrange flowers in white or clear glass vases.

14. Fill white bowls with lemons and limes. They look great and give off a nice scent.

Summer Dressing

Simple and direct is a comfortable style for unfussy summer living. Settle on a theme that includes color and texture with furnishings that are interchangeable when necessary.

Entryway

This area sets the stage for the rest of the house. Green and white are fresh and cool. Add touches of pale peach on wood trim and carry the colors into the other rooms. Use a rag rug here.

Use White Lavishly

To offset any color, use white lavishly. It will create a crisp, clean, summery look. For example, paint all door, window, and wall trim bright white. Where you have wallpaper in the bedrooms, paint the trim white.

Simple Window Treatment

A light and airy window treatment is a simplified version of the traditional poofy balloon shade. Piqué is a wonderful choice of fabric because it has texture and body and at the same time is fresh.

Chair Covers

Cover a bedroom chair in cotton canvas and add the subtle detailing of piping in a color used in the room.

Recycling Is Better Than New

Find ways to recycle existing outdated furniture by giving it paint treatments.

Bed Covers

Cover the bed in pure white with fresh white linens and lace-trimmed accent pillows. Everything will look cool and inviting.

Floor Treatment

If the floors of an old house are in good condition and beautiful, they should be left alone, but if they have been previously painted or are in poor condition, spattering is a wonderful design solution. It is good-looking and practical.

Elegant Dining

A dining room should feel intimate and complement the food. A pale coral or tangerine color flatters both people and food. Again, use white trim everywhere. A nice tabletop treatment is striped fabric in soft green and pink with pure white or damask napkins. Potted herbs will add a faint, fresh scent as a centerpiece. Add lots of candles for a romantic ambience. The reflections of candles in glass hurricane lamps on a windowsill will add sparkle.

All Hands on Deck

With minimal time and effort, homeowners can prepare their decks to look (and feel) their best. It's so liberating to walk from the house to the deck in bare feet...that is, if the deck is smooth. Here are a few handy tips.

No More Splinters

Are there any loose nails or wood splinters around the surface? Reset the nails and sand away the splinters. Don't wait until after you get a splinter in your foot.

Loose Boards

Make sure the wood is sound, then remove the old nails and use new ones to anchor the boards securely.

Waterproof

Clean dirty areas that have nail streaks (dark charcoal gray strip marks that start at the tip of the nail and run straight down). Prevent damage from the elements. Thompson's Water Seal will protect the wood against splitting, cracking, and warping but allow it to weather to a silvery gray.

Deck-orating: Getting the Look You Want

What if you have a brand new deck? Stain is perfect for hiding pressure-treated lumber's green tint. Wait thirty days after the pressure-treatment to ensure optimal stain penetration. Thompson's Water Seal Exterior Stain allows you to waterproof and stain at the same time. And they have over a hundred colors to choose from!

After the Rain

Don't stain if rain is expected within twenty-four hours after application.

No Lap Marks

Avoid lap marks by keeping the leading edge wet and keep working until you reach a corner.

Mix and Match

When staining a large surface, make sure all the batch numbers on the cans match. If you're in the middle of the job and think you'll run out, stop, buy another can, and intermix it if the numbers aren't the same. Mix half the stain from one can with half from the other of the same color.

Aging

Give your new deck an older, weathered look instantly by applying a mixture of one cup household baking soda and one gallon of water to the deck. Let the solution dry, then rinse off and apply a water sealer.

Fences, Shutters, and Exterior Wood

Exterior wood is susceptible to biological damage such as mold, mildew, algae, and rot during warm, moist months. Shaded areas, such as those behind shutters, underneath awnings, and beneath decks, are very vulnerable because the wet surface won't dry as quickly. Here's what to do:

Test for Protection

Sprinkle water around the house on surfaces made of different building materials: brick patios, window boxes, decks, shutters, fences, etc. Does the water bead up? If so, the surface is protected. If the water immediately soaks in or turns the surface darker, then it needs protection.

Seal It Safely

Protect your porch swing and redwood furniture with a water seal waterproofing formula to keep it from warping and cracking. Thompson's is also safe to use on children's outdoor equipment such as jungle gyms.

Other Uses for Sealer

1. Wicker furniture is also susceptible to splitting and cracking and can be waterproofed.
2. Use a waterproofer on a canvas boat cover to help it repel water better and retard mildew.
3. Large areas? Apply a water seal with a garden sprayer.
4. Outdoor statues made with a natural, porous material should also be protected.
5. Give special attention to walkways that collect standing water, and also to the concrete base of a house. If you have an automatic sprinkler system that hits your wooden fence, the fence should be protected with a sealer.

Questions? Call Thompson's team of experts at their toll-free HelpLine seven days a week: 1-800-367-6297.

Nature's Bounty

There are all sorts of natural materials just waiting to be collected and turned into decorative accessories with little or no effort.

Bleached Out

Pinecones, nuts, pine straw, and shells take on a new look when bleached. Equal parts of bleach and water make an easy solution for most natural materials unless they are particularly dark. In this case you would use the bleach at full strength.

Tree Ornament

An especially pretty tree ornament can be made from a single bleached pinecone tied with a red ribbon. This is a nice gift to take to a party during the holidays.

Natural Wreath

Hickory nuts, pecans, and acorns will look entirely different after soaking in bleach. Use these to decorate a dark vine wreath.

Basketful

Bleach a dark basket, then fill it with dried flowers interspersed with baby's breath.

Miniature Wreaths

At our house we make miniature wreaths covered with tiny shells to send when a card isn't enough, but a larger gift isn't appropriate. They are perfect for hanging on the Christmas tree, and they serve as a great reminder in the winter of a walk on the beach on a lazy summer day. Soak small white shells in a bleach solution to clean. A hot glue gun (sold in craft departments and hardware stores) is a great tool for this project. Regular white craft glue will also work but takes longer to dry. Add a generous white satin ribbon bow to the top.

Making Things Cozy

Make your home comfortable and cozy for winter. There are many little changes that anyone can make to create an invitingly warm environment.

Lighting

Lighting is the best way to change the look of things. Keep everything low; not just the wattage, but the height of the lamps as well. Low lighting softens the furnishings in a room the way makeup smooths the wrinkles. Pink light bulbs are an old trick for creating a glow in the bedroom; they make everything look rosier, including people.

Camouflage

Replace small plants with one large plant or tree to make a dramatic statement. Use it to hide a corner of the room that isn't so pretty. If you have a paneled wall that you'd like to replace, cover it with wallpaper. Hang a large painting or group of artwork on the wall to create a main attraction.

Warm Accessories

If you don't have the money to recover or replace an old sofa, throw a quilt or patchwork pillows on it for a comfortable country look. It does wonders toward making a favorite but tired piece even more comfortable.

Carpets

If an area of the carpet is worn, cover it with a small hooked rug. This will add charm, distraction, and interest.

Familiar Surroundings

Cover an unattractive table with an antique lace table cover or pretty fabric and fill the tabletop with framed family photographs. A grouping like this is always comforting to look at and will make the room personal and warm.

Overdo a Good Thing

Most people feel best when surrounded by their cherished things. Take out all your favorite memorabilia and arrange it carefully around the rooms. It will bring you pleasure and give comfort to the soul.

Rearrange Furniture

Change the arrangement for a different flow pattern. Create intimate groupings. Pile books on a table near a comfortable chair. When the weather turns warm you can create a looser arrangement with less clutter on tables. Fresh flowers and a coffee table book on gardens will perk up a tabletop.

Getting Organized

January, a month without holidays once you get past New Year's Day, always seems like a good time to get organized, and there are all sorts of products to help you do this.

Kitchen Clutter

The Rubbermaid company has a cutlery tray with a sliding section and it fits most standard kitchen drawers. There are eleven spacious compartments for storing cutlery, baking utensils, and gadgets. I like to use it for storing arts and crafts or sewing supplies. It's also good for holding cosmetics or office materials.

Work Space

Customize your storage areas with Work Space products by Rubbermaid. These items look like little utility bins or shelves. Each one snaps into a wall strip (part of the system), or they can be mounted on any pegboard or sit on a tabletop or counter. While they are intended for holding tools, paint, etc. in the garage, they have a multitude of uses. Use them to organize socks, underwear, etc. for easy access in a child's room. They are perfect in a sewing room, bathroom, or the inside of a closet door as well.

Stuck No More

Remember when putting Con-Tact Brand adhesive paper on shelves meant getting all wrapped up in the sticky stuff? If you didn't put it down perfectly the first time, you could never pick it up to replace it. And when it was time to change it, you just had to keep piling layers upon layers because you could never get it up again. Those days are over. The new coverings are easy to use and reuse, but best of all the patterns are really nice. You'll find everything from animal farm scenes with black and white cows and denim and cross-stitch country designs to swiss dots, calicos, adorable Victoriana cats, barnwood, and a line of Disney characters. I like the tiny floral prints for covering little tins and boxes.

Special Occasions

Home for New Year's Eve

New Year's Eve is special because it offers hope. It's a moment to reflect on the past and make resolutions for the future. Even if we don't stick to them, on this particular evening our intentions are what counts. And we all have good ones. If you plan to stay home with a loved one on New Year's Eve, make the living room as romantic as possible. In this way whatever words of wisdom you exchange and promises you vow to keep will seem all the more important.

Keep It Soft and Romantic

It doesn't take much to create a room filled with hope for a brighter future. Candles do it for me. Lots and lots of candles. No harsh lights to illuminate reality, such as walls that need painting or slipcovers that could use a cleaning. That is not the stuff upon which a romantic evening is based.

Lovely Scents

Make the room smell like a holiday. All it takes is the scent of pine from the Christmas tree or a bowl filled with pine needles, something warm and delicious simmering on the stove or baking in the oven, and bowls filled with lemons and limes studded with cloves.

Spice It Up

Spice boil bag: Peel around an orange to make a continuous strip of rind. Cut several smaller strips of rind. Place these, along with 1–2 tablespoons of whole cloves and 3 cinnamon sticks, in the center of a square of cheesecloth. Gather the ends of the cheesecloth and gently tie with the long strip of orange rind. Place the bag into 2 cups of water over low heat, or in an uncovered teapot, for 2–3 hours, adding water as needed. The air will be filled with a spicy scent.

Pining for You

If you have a balsam Christmas tree, or one in the yard, gather the fallen needles. They will keep their scent from year to year and act as a room freshener. Fill a basket to have on a table.

In the Mood

Select just the right music before midnight for whatever mood you'd like to create.

Soul Setting

Select your favorite foods and decide where you'd like to eat. Next, set the area with a special flair. For example, use a lacy tablecloth and napkins and your best silver, china, and glasses. Fill a basket with freshly cut greens for the centerpiece.

Sparkle a New Year's Party

If you're having a party on New Year's Eve or New Year's Day, create a sparkling theme with everything silver and gold.

Tablecloth

Use silver mylar for a tablecloth. If you can't find this, tape wrapping paper together to create a silver table cover. Apply gold sticker stars at random, all over the tablecloth.

Centerpiece

Pile small silver and gold balls in a glass bowl and cut pieces of tinsel to arrange here and there among the balls. Wrap a garland of tinsel around the base of the bowl and arrange balls on top all the way around.

All Lit Up

Fill a glass bowl with a string of white Christmas tree lights, set on a sideboard, and hide the cord behind the table.

Candlelight

Arrange silver and gold candles in clear candleholders. Place silver and gold votive candles in goblets or large glasses of different heights and group them together.

Buffet Style

Use red cloth napkins for a buffet and tie the silverware and each napkin together with a gold cord or gold and silver rickrack.

Sparkling Glasses

Serve champagne to go with this theme. Use sparkle glue that comes in a tube to create decorative swirls on the champagne glasses. It will wash off after the party.

Greeting Guests

Fill a basket with bare tree branches, or spray them with silver paint and decorate with large gold and silver stars cut from paper and mounted on cardboard. Place this in the entryway to greet guests.

In an Instant

Arrange clear lights and tinsel wherever you need a bit of sparkle. Wrap houseplants with big silver or gold bows and add tinsel garlands over the tops of curtains like glittering swags.

Decorating for Valentine's Day

Valentine's Day is a perfect holiday because everything about it is simple and straightforward. The theme is romantic, and the colors to use are red and white. It doesn't cost a fortune to remember those you care most about and it doesn't drive you crazy with things to remember to do. In short, it's short and sweet!

A Basket of Flowers

Spray paint a basket white, then sponge red acrylic paint over it. Fill with red and white carnations.

Kisses

Fill a large white bowl with Hershey's kisses. They come wrapped in silver and red foil for Valentine's Day.

Cookie Cutter Appliqué

Use a heart-shaped cookie cutter to mark a heart shape on red fabric (felt won't fray). Cut the same heart shape from fusible webbing such as Stitch Witchery (from fabric shops) and, using a warm iron, apply a heart to one corner of existing placemats.

From Plain to Fancy

Use a heart-shaped cookie cutter and a Magic Marker to add a border of red hearts to plain white napkins.

Love Mats

Cut large, heart-shaped placemats from red construction paper for a one-time use.

Egg-citing

Hard-boil a bunch of white eggs and use markers to draw little red hearts all over them. Arrange in a basket or interesting container. (Make egg salad the next day for lunch!)

A Touch of Color

Group red and white scented candles in strategic spots and place the candleholders on red or white doilies.

Pretty Plant Pots

Tie white ribbons around your plant pots and attach a red paper heart in the center of each bow.

Fresh Flowers

Splurge on a bunch of red and white tulips or sweetheart roses. Place them in a white pitcher or a clear glass vase. There is nothing prettier than fresh flowers in the winter.

Dressing Up

Bring out everything lacy and white and romantic such as tablecloths, napkins, pillowcases, guest towels, and good china and silverware and dress up the house for a Valentine's dinner at home.

Winter Party

If the winter blues have gotten to you, a party is an excuse to dress up the house and make you feel better. Even if you live in a warm climate, it's fun to create a winter scene for a "no reason at all" get-together.

Winter Wonderland

With a little patience you can create the most wonderful party environment for practically no money. It takes time, but it's a cinch to fabricate a winter wonderland with make-believe snowflakes. Here's how to do it.

Use a sewing needle and nylon filament to string those little foam popcorn pellets used for packing delicate objects, and hang them from the ceiling. Fill the entire room so it looks as though snowflakes are suspended in air just above head height. Any movement in the air will cause the white popcorn to move and sway about as if snow were really falling.

Tabletops

Keep everything winter green and white. Cover tabletops with white cloth and use white lace-edged napkins. If you want sparkle, sprinkle handfuls of gold and silver sparkle dust over the top.

Centerpiece

Fill a white ceramic bowl with branches of evergreens and sprinkle with handfuls of Ivory Snow flakes to simulate snow on the branches. Surround the bowl with loose handfuls of Poly-Fil stuffing (five-and-ten-cent stores carry it by the bagful) to look like mounds of snow.

Egg-citing Ideas for Easter

Create unusual eggs for a delightful and spirited centerpiece for the holiday table.

Marbleize

For sophisticated egg dyers there's a kit for marbleizing gorgeous eggs in minutes. And they're edible! Use one color for each egg rather than the multicolors the kids will surely find appealing. Fill a beautiful porcelain or ceramic dish with these eggs rather than placing them on a bed of green "grass" as in the usual Easter basket. Add mismatched floral napkins to the table for a springlike bouquet. Remnants of fabrics are great for making napkin squares.

Tie-Dyed

The plain, old-fashioned egg dyes are always reliable and the colors are brilliant. Nothing says Easter like those bright fuchsia, electric blue, and passionate purple colors. Use these colors for a tie-dye effect. Before dipping each egg into the dye, wrap it with string. Just wrap the string around the egg one way, then the other, and around again in another direction and tie, leaving a length of string for dunking. Dip the egg into the dye as usual, then remove. Let dry and when the string is removed these areas will be white. Or you can wrap the egg with crisscrossing rubber bands (carefully) for the same effect.

Sponge It!

For a sponging technique without paint or dyes, wad up a piece of colored tissue paper, dampen, and dab onto the egg. The color will come off, giving the white egg a dappled, delicate sponging effect. Let dry before handling.

A Blooming Basket

Once you've got the eggs decorated you'll need a container for the centerpiece. Take a plain loose-weave basket and weave flowers and ribbons in and out of the reeds around the base and through the handles. Freesia and honeysuckle are nice with daffodils, daisies, and roses. Gracefully wind vines of ivy along the top rim of the basket and around the handle. Insert sprigs of airy filler such as baby's breath behind the flowers. Fill the basket with a lacy doily or napkin and some greens. Then arrange chocolate bunnies in the basket with the eggs.

Gift Baskets for Mother's Day

For a personalized Mother's Day gift, choose a theme related to your mother's interests and fill a basket with appropriate things. Baskets come in all sizes and shapes and different styles can be used for different objects. Some baskets are already decorated with stencil designs or ribbons, some are painted, but most are plain, the interest coming from their shape or materials. Some have handles while others don't. If you want to decorate the basket before filling it, this will enhance its use after the gifts within have been used.

Small Plants

Fill a round or square low basket with small pots of African violets and add Spanish moss to unify the pots. Tie a fat satin ribbon around the basket, or around the handle if it has one. If your mother enjoys cooking, fill a willow basket with small herb plants for the kitchen.

For the Gardener

Some baskets have compartments. These are great for giving gardening accessories. Fill each section with a good pair of clippers, garden gloves, packets of seeds, potting soil, and floral note cards.

For the New Mom

If you're a new father, make a hit with a basket from your newborn to the new mom for her first Mother's Day.

Choose a pretty pastel basket and fill it with such items as a framed picture of the new baby, a "baby's first" record book, a bottle of perfume or something silky and sexy, and the May issue of *Parents* magazine.

For the Sewer

Make a personalized sewing basket filled with all sorts of notions such as a pin cushion, pins, a new pair of scissors, and a pattern to make something she'd love along with the fabric to make it, and tie the handle with a fat bow made from a tape measure.

For the Crafter

For the quilter fill a basket with a variety of fabric remnants, a rotary cutter, needle holders, and a quilt pattern. For the knitter or crocheter fill a basket with beautiful yarn and a pattern to make a sweater or afghan.

To Pamper Her

A day of pampering includes a basket filled with fancy soap, bath oil beads, a loofa mitt, body cream, shampoo, cream rinse, and a romantic novel to read in the tub.

A Month of Reading

If your mom loves to pore over magazines, fill a basket with the latest issue of every magazine you think she'd like. Add a box of her favorite chocolates or fresh fruit.

Closet Queen

Line a basket with a new bath towel and fill it with individually rolled hand towels tied with pretty ribbons. Add a set of padded hangers, scented shoe stuffers, a set of lingerie cases, and a container of potpourri.

For the Cook

Fill a basket with luxuries one doesn't usually buy for oneself. The possibilities are enormous, from cooking utensils to cookbooks to specialty food items from a gourmet shop.

Spice It Up

If your mom likes exotic cooking, fill a basket with unusual spices, herbs, and condiments.

For the Tea Lover

Choose a variety of fancy teas, a book about tea, a pretty teacup and saucer, and a box of tea crackers, or homemade cookies and special jam.

For the Coffee Lover

Buy small packages of a variety of freshly ground coffees. Fill the basket with espresso, mocha bean candies, and other coffee-flavored goodies.

From Kids to Mom

Guaranteed to be appreciated. Design a bunch of cards with promised favors enclosed, such as "This ticket is good for____." You fill in the personalized favor that will make your mom happy or make life a bit easier for her. Put each one in an envelope and decorate the outside. Fill the basket with colored tissue paper and insert the envelopes on end between the tissue folds so it looks interesting. Tie with a pretty ribbon and streamers, maybe even a few balloons, and insert a fresh flower into the basket.

At-Home Picnic

Warm any mom's heart with a picnic basket filled with a bottle of wine, a complete take-out dinner, and a rented movie.

Wedding Treasures

Handmade items make special wedding gifts or keepsakes for your wedding party. There's a lovely saying to keep in mind: "Today's pleasures are tomorrow's treasures."

Wedding Ring Quilt

Truly a gift of love, this is a present the couple will still be using when they have grandchildren and, with care, will be passed on to future generations in the family. If you can't afford a full-size quilt, a small wallhanging in this or a Double Wedding Ring pattern is pretty enough to hang on the wall. If you enjoy quilting, this is the pattern to choose, and you can make it in the colors to match their bedroom.

Afghan

No newlyweds should be without a granny square crocheted afghan to warm their home and hearth. A handmade afghan is a gift for all time.

For the Bridesmaids

Give each of your best friends a handmade gift as a special remembrance of your wedding. A craft item such as a cross-stitch framed saying, a small piece of pottery, a one-of-a-kind pair of silver earrings, or a wooden box can be found at craft fairs or shops. Don't forget your mother and his.

Making the Decorations

You might like to make some of the decorations for your wedding. Depending on the time of year, all sorts of natural materials are readily available for creating your own centerpiece. Top the wedding cake with handcrafted miniature bride and groom dolls. After the wedding, keep these to hang as ornaments on your first Christmas tree.

Stenciling

Decorate a small piece of unfinished furniture, such as a blanket chest. It can be stained, marbleized, or sponge painted. Then stencil your names and date on the front and varnish it for protection.

Personalized Ornament

If you are the mother of the bride or groom, consider making a special ornament to give to the couple at the rehearsal dinner. This will start a tradition of giving the newlyweds a special ornament each year on their anniversary or for Christmas. We do this in our family for weddings and births and have discovered this is how future heirlooms are born.

Ring Pillow

This little accessory is fun to make. It can be as elaborate as you want. Stitch two lacy handkerchiefs together and stuff. Then add a wide eyelet trim with satin ribbon all around the edge. After the wedding, use this as a little accessory pillow on your bed.

Preserving the Wedding Invitation

Many of you enjoy doing one craft or another, and it's easy to use these techniques to preserve the wedding invitation for a most treasured gift.

Cross-Stitch

Make a wedding sampler by duplicating the invitation in stitches with counted cross-stitch. Craft shops carry the supplies and will have a charted alphabet so you can create the names of the bride and groom and the marriage date. Determine the finished size of the cross-stitched invitation and cut a piece of even-weave Aida cloth to size. It should fit into a standard frame. Next, center the names and date on the cloth and then surround it with flowers or a ribbon tied at the top with a bow. There are many charted designs to choose from in booklets or kits made especially for this purpose.

Decoupage

Mount the invitation on a tray, box, or plaque. Begin by painting the object. Position the invitation on the item and glue in place. Cut out pretty flowers from greeting cards, a print, wrapping paper, or a book. Arrange the flowers so they surround and slightly overlap the edges of the invitation and glue all around. Let dry and apply several coats of polyurethane. If you've made a plaque, add a hanging brass picture frame hook to the top.

Pressed Flowers

Press some of the flowers from the centerpiece at a wedding and use them to decorate the outside edges around the invitation and set in a frame.

Picture Album

Decorate the front of an album with the wedding invitation. Frame it with a narrow satin or velvet ribbon glued around the edge of the invitation. Start the album with some candid photos of the couple before they were a couple, maybe baby pictures supplied by their parents. But remember, nothing embarrassing!

An Informal Wedding Party

There's nothing more intimate than an at-home wedding with family and close friends. If it's a summer wedding an outdoor party is relaxing for everyone. Decorations can be less formal, taking advantage of the natural setting. You might also use these decorations for a bridal shower.

Pots of Pink

Dress up clay pots with sponge painting in white over the red clay and fill with lots of pink geraniums and impatiens. Trim the rim of each pot with lacy doily shelf trim to create a delicate finishing touch. Add Queen Anne's lace to the pots at the last minute. The paper doily trim, called Doily Carte, is carried by Wolfman-Gold & Good Company in New York City (or see page 328 to order by mail).

Centerpieces

Arrange a country basket filled with Queen Anne's lace for the buffet table. It's so bride-like and abundantly available. Or cover pots of miniature topiaries with a pretty floral fabric to match the tablecloths.

Table Covers

Choose one fabric or two corresponding fabrics to create the theme for your party and use it everywhere. Pink roses are always a favorite and Laura Ashley's Rose Trellis pattern is a classic in pink and white. Combine this with their pink and white stripe or overall rosebud print. In addition to table covers, cover seat cushions on outdoor furniture and cut strips to tie fat bows on outdoor chairs to dress them up for the occasion.

Umbrellas

If you have umbrella tables on the patio or lawn, make fabric covers with scalloped edges. No sewing is involved. Use pinking shears so edges don't ravel and look messy. Add fabric bows between scallops. Chances are your outdoor umbrellas are a bit dirty this time of year, and this cover-up saves messy cleanup for the end of summer.

Festive Touches

Dress up the front door to welcome guests with a festive decoration. Add wildflowers and grasses to a wreath of natural vines. Baby's breath is pretty here too.

Day into Night

If your party starts in the late afternoon and continues beyond sundown, provide romantic lighting with candles in glass containers on all the tables. Fat white candles in snifters; votives grouped in small glass containers; hurricane lamps over tall, fat candles; and candles in large glasses—you can't have too many.

Romantic Interlude

If your garden is in bloom it may be the only color needed as a background. Use white lavishly. Cover tables in white damask, use white lace-edged napkins and white flowers on the tables. A buffet is more appropriate for an informal gathering. Cover the table with antique lace and fill a large, country basket with white cosmos, Queen Anne's lace, and other wildflowers.

Picnic Party Tips

There are lots of products on the market that go well with a picnic or outdoor party. They are nicer than the usual paper fare and can be used indoors as well. Since we are all ecology-conscious it makes sense to save the money from buying paper throwaway goods and invest it in a longer-lasting product.

Glassware

You'll find Rubbermaid's line of inexpensive plastic glasses in most supermarkets. They are lightweight but as thick as Lucite, and until you actually lift one you can't tell it from the real thing. They come in two sizes in clear, or with a smoky gray or pink cast. This is a far cry from the paper or plastic glasses associated with picnicking, and while you can't toss them away afterward, they won't break if dropped, they're dishwasher safe, and they will last forever.

Chinaware

All-white plastic dishes are much nicer for a picnic than paper plates and are worth the investment as you can use them over and over again. They come in dinner and luncheon sizes and in pink or blue as well, but the white looks more like real chinaware. They are quite practical for everyday kidproof use, or save them for the next party. A plastic plate may be unacceptable for a dinner party but it adds substance to a picnic when paper plates are expected.

Cloth Napkins

Large cloth napkins are easy to toss in the washing machine after a party and are much nicer to use than paper. Different colored bandanas make colorful napkins. Tie one around each person's set of utensils. Or cut 16-inch cotton squares with pinking shears to make no-sew napkins for a picnic.

Table Cover with a Country Flair

For a country theme cover the table with a patchwork quilt. If you shudder at the thought, remember, quilts were originally made to be used and can withstand repeated washings.

Hold Everything

Large country baskets are perfect for holding just about everything. Line the bread basket with a lace-edged linen cloth or a colorful napkin. Choose pretty fabrics or linens to line baskets for salads, etc. and then place a dish or bowl inside to hold the food and protect any delicate fabrics. No picnic would be complete without a basket brimming with fruit, which can also serve as a centerpiece.

Centerpiece

While the food is enough of a centerpiece for the table, it's still nice to cluster a few pots of impatiens in a basket or create a casual bouquet of wildflowers. I like an all-white table and a basket filled with white cosmos, Queen Anne's lace, white freesia, and baby gladiolus. There is just enough green to set off the white against the dark vines of the basket.

Pretty Food

Plan the food so the colors are pleasing. Use edible flowers for decorating colorless plates of chicken and such. Nasturtium surrounding the meat or deviled eggs, for example, adds color where needed, as do basil leaves surrounding slices of tomato.

Cooling the Drinks

Everyone uses coolers or trash cans to hold ice and cold drinks, but why not decorate a new metal trash can for the occasion? Self-adhesive borders are perfect to wrap around the can, or you can cut out large petals and stems from plain self-adhesive shelf paper to create flowers growing around the can. To dress up the can, first spray paint it white, then add the decorations.

Farewell to Bugs

To keep mosquitoes away, attach long citronella candles to garden stakes and plant in the ground around the area. This adds a festive glow to the party as the sun sets.

Poolside Picnic

Designer Raymond Waites is fond of using a small child's red wagon to hold all sorts of items for his poolside parties. One year he rolled out lobsters on a bed of ice. Another year the wagon held ice chilling cans of soda, and at another time it held pots of flowers.

Just for the Fun of It

For a family picnic, frame old baby pictures and intersperse around the food or make a grouping in the center of the table. Your guests will have fun identifying themselves.

Halloween Decorations

Halloween is an exciting holiday for children and provides an excuse to spruce up the house with a fall theme that includes some bright orange and spooky black.

Window Decorations

Plastic canvas is sold in hobby stores for needlepoint projects. It's stiff and can be cut into shapes. The holes are large so it takes seconds to stitch. Use a Magic Marker to draw shapes onto it, then fill in with yarn stitches and cut out. Make pumpkins to hang in the window, or cut four pumpkin shapes and stitch together at the edges to create a box for a centerpiece. Each side is stitched with orange, black, and green (for the stem) and the center can be filled with a plant or dried branches.

Pipe Cleaner Tree

Make a Halloween tree with black pipe cleaners. Insert several pipe cleaners into a florist's block for the base. Then wrap more pipe cleaners around the upright cleaners to create a bent and gnarled trunk. Make branches by attaching and twisting pipe cleaners into different shapes. Wrap small bundles of candy in orange fabric or napkins and tie with orange ribbons to hang from the branches.

Fall Centerpiece

Cover the center of your table with leaves and place a decorated pumpkin in the center. Or make a family of three different-sized pumpkins, each decorated accordingly with black markers. Add curly ribbon hair to the top of one and glue bushy yarn eyebrows to another or use sequins, beads, buttons, and other odds and ends for your creations.

Creative Candleholders

Group tiny pumpkins together as candleholders. Cut a hole in the top of each, large enough to insert a candle. Line them up on the windowsill. No pumpkin carving is needed.

Ribbon Pumpkin

For an elegant centerpiece, begin with a large Styrofoam ball. Cut strips of different shades of orange ribbon long enough to wrap from the top to the bottom of the ball. Attach one end with a pin into the top of the Styrofoam and bring the other end to the opposite side. Attach with another pin. Continue to wrap the ball in this way with alternating shades of color. Cut felt leaves and a stem and attach to the top of the pumpkin with pins. Or use ribbon that can be curled by firmly drawing it over a scissors to make a clump of green for the top. Curl ribbon over a pencil and attach for trailing vines. If you can't find a large enough Styrofoam ball, make several small pumpkins.

15-Minute Decoration

Weave orange and black ribbons through a loose-reed basket and fill with candy corn. Tie the handle with a large crepe paper bow and set it in a visible place.

Theme
Party

If you've traveled to a particular place, why not share it with friends and relive the experience in a new way? Here are ten tips for how it's done:

1. Send out invitations on postcards from the place you traveled to.
2. Decorate with travel posters.
3. Write for brochures from the tourist organization representing the area and put these at each person's place on the table as a souvenir.
4. Take out travel books of the area from the library to place on the coffee table.
5. Use maps to make placemats or arrange souvenir items in the center of the table. To make a placemat, cut the maps into 12 x 14-inch pieces. Cover with clear Con-Tact paper.
6. Use napkins in the national colors of the country and tie each with ribbons of the appropriate color.

7. If the theme is a foreign country, get a music tape of the country to play in the background and set the mood.

8. Every country has its special food. Make an event of the meal and make the food as authentic as you can.

9. If it's possible, choose flowers of the country you visited. Arrange in interesting bunches around the room.

10. Plan a slide show for after dinner. Be selective and edit your slides so the show will be lively. Keep the slides moving at a nice clip so your guests are entertained. Try to remember not to linger on a favorite spot and digress into a long story about the place. Make it more show than tell. A good rule of thumb is 45 minutes in all.

Thanksgiving Table Dressing

Thanksgiving is another perfect holiday. It's reliable. It's always on a Thursday no matter what year it is. You can count on exactly one day of gorging out. There's no month-long buildup to drive us crazy, and besides preparing the meal, there really is only one other thing to do and that's dress the table. Think about it before you're knee-deep in cranberry sauce.

Rich with Tapestry

Tapestry is the most wonderful texture for a Thanksgiving table cover. The earth tones make a rich background for the holiday food. If you can't find one you can afford, or one that is large enough to fit your table, buy a smaller one to place over the center of a larger tablecloth. You can also make your own. Buy the tapestry in a shop that sells upholstery fabric. It comes wider than most cottons and polyesters. Cut the cloth so that it fits the top of your table with a few inches hanging down. Finish the edges with a pretty braid or wide decorative ribbon border all around.

7 Quick and Easy Centerpieces

1. Fill a basket with fruits and nuts and scatter some of the nuts around the basket on the table.
2. Make an arrangement of different-sized pumpkins, gourds, and squash. Scatter a few leaves around the centerpiece and add orange, brown, or dark green candles.
3. Cut the tops off small pumpkins and scoop out the centers. Place votive candles inside and make a grouping.
4. Make a bed of pine needles in the center of the table. Fill a basket with pinecones and tie a brown plaid taffeta ribbon bow on the handle.
5. Make floating walnut candles: Scoop out the meat from walnuts and set aside the shells. Melt the stubs of old candles in a coffee can set in a pan of water on the stove. If you place the shells in a pan of sand it will be easy to fill each one without dripping wax on your hand. Use a short wick and hold upright in the center of each shell as you fill it with the melted wax. Float the candles in a pretty bowl filled with water.
6. Fill a bowl with water and float the tops of flowers

such as chrysanthemums or marigolds. Surround with candles in fall colors.

7. Instead of a centerpiece, create a tiny arrangement of fall flowers in little vases, cups, or glasses at each person's place. Use calico napkins in fall colors and tie each one with a ribbon. Tuck a flower under each ribbon bow.

50 Night-Before-Christmas Ideas That Don't Look It

It's Christmas Eve and all your good crafting and decorating intentions are spread in pieces before you; the half-finished dress for the baby, twenty-four ornaments finished but lacking hoops for hanging, and tons of ideas that never happened. It's time for some last-minute ideas that don't look thrown together. Chances are you can create an instant display from items that are right in your home or by using greens from the backyard.

Sparkle Plenty

Fill the room with candles at different heights. Use clear jars, drinking glasses, and wine glasses to hold votive candles.

Nature's Way

Use fruit such as pears and apples for candlesticks. Polish red delicious and green Granny Smith apples and cut a hole through the top. Insert a small red or white candle in each. Line them on the windowsill or cluster them on a table.

Greet Guests with a Glow

Create a welcome glow in the hallway. Loop a wide plaid taffeta ribbon around a wreath of greens and place it on a table. Fill the center with fat red candles of varying heights.

Stairway Greenery

If you have a stairway, gather a large spray of greens, such as boxwood, with a generous bow and wire it to the banister. Add a few small Christmas balls to the greens and it will look as good as a bough purchased at a nursery.

Silver Branches

Create a mini-tree of spray-painted branches stuck into a large clay pot or pretty container. String with tiny white lights for a welcome at the front door.

Welcome Banner

Use glue and colored felt to create a welcome banner. Draw a design of holly leaves and berries and cut each piece from green and red felt. Arrange and glue to the center of a rectangular piece of fabric the size desired for your banner. Then draw block letters to spell *Cheers* or *Noel* and use these patterns to cut the letters from felt. Glue to the fabric background just above the berry design and hang the banner with Velcro tabs.

Spicy Scents

Pierce lemons and limes around the middle with cloves and set them in clay saucers. Do the same with red and green polished apples in a wooden salad bowl. Fill a small vase or basket with cinnamon sticks tied with red plaid ribbons. Simmer cinnamon in boiling water on the stove when your guests arrive. The air will be nicely scented with the smells of Christmas.

Sachets

Use squares of Christmas fabric remnants to make sachets. Fill the center of each square with your favorite potpourri mix, gather the ends of the fabric, and tie with pretty ribbon or satin cord. Fill a basket and give one to everyone who stops by during the holiday week.

Bejeweled Tree Ornaments

Use empty thread spools, coat with glitter glue, and add bits of gems and beads around the center. Thread a fat gold cord through the hole and hang near the lights so they'll glitter.

Medieval Ornamentation

Insert a variety of brass tacks and nails into Styrofoam balls so the balls are completely encrusted. These ornaments are too heavy to hang on the tree, but two or three in a glass bowl create a fabulous table decoration.

Sparkle Stars

For quick and easy ornaments use a cookie cutter to cut stars from Styrofoam. Coat the cut edges and one side with glitter glue. Let dry and do the reverse side. With a needle and embroidery thread or gold cord weave through the end of one point to create a loop for hanging.

Display Your Christmas Cards

Punch a hole in each card you've received and hang with a ribbon on the spray-painted branches from the suggestion on page 312.

Pretty Boxes

Cover a cardboard box with bits of lace, ribbon, doilies, and buttons to hold a gift. The box then becomes as special as the gift.

Out of Wrapping Paper?

If you're in the middle of wrapping gifts and have suddenly run out of paper, silver foil or pretty shelf paper is just as festive. Old maps make an interesting wrap.

Paper Bag Wrapping

If you're really stuck for wrapping paper, open and cut a paper bag down one side. Cut off the bottom and iron it flat. Use cookie cutters and crayons or colorful markers to stencil an overall design on the brown paper.

Lapnaps

For buffet dining, oversized napkins are practical and are prettier than paper ones. Cut large pieces of fabric with pinking shears. No hemming is needed, and they won't fray.

Buffet Dining

Roll each place setting of silverware in white napkins and tie with fat red yarn bows or velvet ribbon. Insert a sprig of greens or a stick of cinnamon under each tie.

Centerpiece

Mushroom baskets from the supermarket make wonderful centerpiece holders. Fill the inside with a bed of greens, then pile colorful Christmas tree balls on top. Tie a wide ribbon around the rim and add a fat bow at each end. Lace ribbon is especially pretty. Add a sprig of baby's breath, holly, or mistletoe under each bow.

Dress Your Plants

Tie ribbons around your houseplants. Add tiny lace bows tied to branches, or cut 2-inch-wide strips of red and white gingham to make country bows. Use these strips to tie packages as well.

Tiny Lights

Fill a glass bowl with a string of tiny tree lights. Conceal the cord behind the table or sideboard. Blinking lights add sparkle.

A Spot of Color

Fill a small country basket, pewter plate, or plain white bowl with fresh cranberries. Stick a sprig or two of holly into the bowl as well.

Decorate the Windows

Combine wide white eyelet with 2-inch-wide red ribbons and make bows with streamers to tie on the ends of curtain rods at each window.

Quick Wreath

Cut out a cardboard wreath and cover it with quilt batting. Wrap the wreath with green checked or calico fabric. Add a big bow at the top and hang in the entryway or over your fireplace.

Playful Scene

Group children's toys around the tree for a playful scene. Tie a pretty ribbon around the neck of an old teddy bear. Sit a doll on a child's chair and arrange blocks, pull toys, even books in a decorative way.

Seeing Red!

Bring out everything red and arrange them around the room. Fill a basket with red balls of yarn and place it on a tabletop. Place shiny apples in a colander or mixing bowl on the kitchen counter. Use a piece of red fabric as an overcloth on top of a white tablecloth. Fill a red mug with peppermint sticks and tie each with a red ribbon. Look through the house for anything red—a plastic mixing spoon, a measuring cup, a pot holder, a red scarf or belt—and use in a clever arrangement.

Temporary Pillow Covers

Cover existing throw pillows with a mix of red printed fabrics. Stitch a front and back piece together, leaving one end open. Slip the pillow inside and pin the opening together. It will be easy to remove the covers after the holidays.

Mantel Display

Fill small, shiny paper gift bags with colored tissue and sprigs of greens for a mantel display.

Cooling It!

Wrap the wine cooler with red fabric and add a plaid taffeta ribbon around the rim.

Lined with Red

When serving crackers with a dip, fill the cracker basket with a red plaid napkin or piece of fabric.

Silver Boxes

Wrap little empty boxes with silver foil and tie with pretty ribbons and a bell in each bow. Group them on a side table, on the windowsill, or around the candles on a buffet table.

Party Apron

Stitch a strip of fabric or ribbon long enough to tie around your waist to the top of a red and white plaid dishtowel for an instant apron. If you have a piece of taffeta fabric, all the better.

Blooming Bandbox

Fill a fabric- or paper-covered bandbox with an arrangement of dried flowers. Add some vegetables as well, such as bunches of broccoli, red and green peppers, and mushrooms.

Not for Cookies Alone

Fill a bowl with shiny cookie cutters and place on a bright patchwork table cover.

To Catch the Light

For a truly instant display, remove labels from small juice bottles with hot water and fill them with water colored with red and green food coloring. Line them up on a window sill. Tie a red taffeta ribbon around the neck of each bottle.

Colored Pinecones

Spray paint a bunch of pinecones red and pile them into a rustic basket. Tie the handle with a pretty bow and set next to the fireplace.

Tieback Gracefully

String cranberries to use as curtain tiebacks. Cut a strip of fabric to place around the curtain over which you'll add the strand of cranberries so they won't stain the curtain.

Red Roses

Arrange boughs of greens on the mantel, then fashion red roses with tissue paper you simply roll and tie at the base. Arrange the roses on the greens.

Gingerbread Men

Fill a doily-lined basket with gingerbread cookies for your centerpiece.

Pine Scents

Cut 4-inch squares of plaid dishtowel fabric or homespun and stitch two together to make a small pillow. Leave one side open and fill with pine needles. Stitch opening closed and fill a basket with these little pillows.

Wheat

Tie stalks of wheat with a muslin or lace bow and place on a table or in a basket.

Clear and Simple

Fill clear glass jars and bottles with water and insert a sprig of evergreens, a branch of Scotch pine, or a sprig of holly in each one. Tie a gold or silver ribbon around the neck of the bottles.

Watering Can-Do

Use a metal watering can to hold an arrangement of greens or flowers.

Under Wraps

Arrange bay leaves around glass votive candles and tie with a ribbon or rope for a rustic decoration. Place one candle at each place setting.

For the Birds

Fill a basket with Spanish moss and arrange small artificial birds on top with wooden eggs interspersed.

Last-Minute Placecards

Write each person's name on a Christmas tree ball using sparkle paint in a tube or Magic Marker and place at each setting.

Star Light, Star Bright

Stencil gold and silver stars over red napkins and tablecloth.

Candy Jars

Fill apothecary jars with Christmas candy. Cut a square of fabric to cover the tops and secure with a ribbon on each. Group them on a table.

Glitter Fruit

Coat fruit such as pears or a cluster of grapes with egg white and roll in silver or gold glitter. Arrange in a porcelain or silver dish on a sideboard.

Mixed Up for the Table

Fill a wooden salad bowl or rustic container with a mixture of assorted greens, pinecones, and berries from your backyard or woods. Mix in some dried flowers and cinnamon sticks and toss as you would a salad. Use as a centerpiece.

Christmas Cookies

If you've made Christmas cookies, put one for each guest in a tiny jewelry box and wrap them up for display under a miniature tree in the hallway. As the guests leave, give each one of the "gifts."

Quilting for Christmas

Christmas is an added incentive for quilters to dig into the scrap basket. The Fairfield Processing Corporation makes quilt batting in a variety of thicknesses and sizes for different uses. The cotton batting is used for baby quilts, wallhangings, and stockings, while "traditional" batting is better for full-size bed quilts. Their stuffing is perfect for ornaments.

Miniatures

Small quilts have become popular as wallhangings or for framing. A group of quilted squares is especially nice in a child's room, on a bathroom wall, or lining a hallway.

Patchwork Stockings

Stitch together 2-inch squares of red and white fabric to make a cloth large enough to cut out a stocking pattern. Use a solid red for the backing. This is a strong design that can look contemporary as well as country-style. Use the scraps to make small ornaments to match.

Pillows

Quilted pillows are quick and easy projects and almost any patchwork pattern can be adapted for this. Pillows can be made in various shapes such as hearts, animals, and other country symbols.

Star Ornaments

Use strips of fabric or ribbons to make pretty star ornaments. They are also great for selling at Christmas bazaars. You'll need a piece of 8-inch-square muslin for the front and one for the back, stuffing, and a batch of ribbons in different colors and widths. Arrange strips of ribbons across one piece of muslin and pin in place. Machine stitch along each ribbon edge. Draw a star pattern on plain paper the same size as the muslin square and cut out. Pin this to the ribbon fabric and the extra piece of muslin and cut out. With right sides facing, pin the fabric pieces together and stitch around, leaving one side of one point open for turning. Clip into the points and turn right side out. Stuff and stitch opening closed. Stitch ribbon or embroidery floss to the tip of one point for hanging.

Crafting for Bazaars

People love to find bargains at bazaars while contributing to a worthy cause. Everyone goes home happy. The most popular bazaar items are country accessories made from scraps of fabric. They should be quick, easy, and inexpensive to make. Use one pattern and make a number of items with different fabrics for variety. The cost is minimal and the items can therefore be reasonably priced.

Mini-Projects

Use small amounts of homespun or calico fabric to make miniature pillows, sachets, pot holders, and padded hangers.

Add a Country Appliqué

Add a country appliqué, such as a heart, watermelon slice, or an apple, to a pot holder and you have an instant winner. Consider making these familiar items from unexpected, extra-pretty fabrics to give them a new look.

Personal Items

Cosmetic and lingerie bags are nice in velvet, moiré, satin, or brocade. Save the calico scraps for quilts. Take the time to add lace and ribbon edgings to sachets and little stocking ornaments.

Country Pillows

Stuffed pillows in the shapes of a pig, whale, swan, cat, and elephant are delightfully country in calico, or are more elegant when made with floral chintz. These projects are easy to make in quantity. Add lace or ribbon trimmings for interest.

Tree Ornaments

Tree ornaments are always popular at bazaars. Get out all your scraps of felt, calico, and ribbons. One of my favorite ornaments is the ribbon star. It's colorful and a cinch to make in quantity, so you can fill the tree or sell them in sets. See page 321. These ornaments will make a delightful display at your bazaar booth and will sell like hotcakes.

Flowers for the Holidays

Cut flowers, flowering plants, greens, and pine branches all add to the holiday fare. The house comes alive and smells like Christmas. What kinds to buy and how to display and arrange them are worth planning before you rush out.

For the Mantelpiece

1. Arrange pine branches across the shelf so they overlap and hang over the edge slightly. No matter how haphazardly you arrange them, they will look great. Furthermore, the room will smell wonderful.
2. Next, add small silver and gold Christmas balls here and there among the boughs. Wrap small jewelry boxes with silver or gold paper and tie with lace ribbons. Arrange these on the pine branches as well.
3. Or, for a country theme, wrap the boxes with plaid taffeta and use bright red or green satin ribbons. Insert a tiny sprig of pine needles under each bow.
4. Add pinecones in various sizes.
5. For sparkle, arrange a garland of tinsel or tiny tree lights in and around the greens. For a country theme, use a garland of cranberries.

Poinsettias

These plants are carefree, last a long time, and always say "Christmas." Buy several in different sizes and group them for impact in a hallway or on a side table. If you use them as a dining table centerpiece, arrange red tapered candles in tall candlesticks along with the plants.

Line a large, country-style basket with plastic to hold several individual plants. Add Spanish moss (available from a florist) over the top of each pot. This will make them appear uniform and as though they'd been planted in the basket. Set the basket on the floor next to the fireplace.

Basket of Greens

Large, full arrangements of greens look best in country baskets. I often sponge paint the surface of a basket for added interest. This is easy to do. You will need a flat, even-weave basket. It might have a handle on which you can later add a decorative bow. Spray paint the outside with white Krylon, fast-drying paint. Using a piece of sponge, dab green acrylic paint at random all over the basket.

Flowering Basket

Decorate a basket with a pretty flower cut from fabric. Glue the cutout onto the front of the basket so that it molds to the weave. Let dry. Add more flowers if desired. Fill the basket with eucalyptus and baby's breath for a delicate country arrangement.

Clear and Dramatic

Fill glass bowls or tall white vases with a dozen or more all-red or all-white tulips. Don't combine them with anything, and use them everywhere. You can't overdo a good thing.

Grow Your Own

Paperwhites are also refreshing. Florists often have kits complete with the shallow pot, soil, pebbles, and bulbs. It's a cinch to create this lovely breath of spring in winter. Fill the pot with soil, place the bulbs on top, and surround with the pebbles. Soak the soil with water and the bulbs do the rest. You can almost watch them grow. I like three pots placed in a row along the back of a kitchen counter, down the center of a breakfast table, or lined up on a windowsill. Create a miniature holiday scene around the base of the pots, using small toys such as a teddy bear, houses, blocks, a sled, whatever you can find. After the holidays you can still enjoy the plants.

Personalize a Wreath

The front door is a good place to start welcoming the holiday season. Flower shops all have fresh garlands and wreaths and it's easy to add your own decorations.

By the Seashore

Collect a variety of shells. Use a hot glue gun to adhere them in clusters around a wreath made of honeysuckle or grapevines.

Romantic Inspiration

Use lace bows, dried rosebuds, and baby's breath to decorate greens or grapevines for a romantic wreath.

Country Style

Make bows of red and white homespun fabric cut with pinking shears and wire to your wreath. Then add miniature toys such as a teddy bear, little red wagon, rag doll, and other small country ornaments.

Traditional

Fat bows of tartan satin ribbon are classic. If you want to go natural, use a base of honeysuckle vines and wire nuts and pinecones all around. Then add a little bird or seagull to the scene.

Simple Elegance

For pure simplicity, tie a bunch of pine branches together with a large bow and hang on the front door. For a more festive look use branches of holly berry.

A White Christmas

Decorating for Christmas doesn't have to mean bright red and green accessories. It doesn't always have to include sparkling gold balls and silvery tinsel. Sometimes it's a relief to remove all extra color from a room and add white accessories.

Trim-a-Tree

Cover the tree with fat white bows made from lace or wide satin ribbon. The contrast of white against the green boughs is quite elegant.

White Sprigs

Spray paint sprigs of tree branches white. Set them into a block of florist's Styrofoam placed in the bottom of a whitewashed basket. Trim the branches with tiny clear tree lights.

Purity on the Table

For the dining area, use a white damask tablecloth with a white crocheted overcloth. Use tall white tapered candles in natural wood or ceramic candlesticks. Fill a large white bowl with sprigs of bayberry branches for a centerpiece.

Candles

Surround the centerpiece with short, fat white candles placed into brandy glasses, fruit compote glass containers, or wide drinking glasses of varying heights. Use lots of them for romantic lighting when entertaining. Group several on a coffee table or sideboard so you have candlelight everywhere. It's very festive and often creates a diversion if what you'd really like to do is reupholster all the furniture.

For the Food

White serving containers set the food off nicely and, when possible, use natural-colored baskets as well. Fill a country basket with a white linen napkin to hold bread or rolls.

Linen Trims

For a guest bedroom, trim pillowcases and the top sheet with 4-inch-wide white eyelet, purchased in fabric stores. This will make ordinary linens special and will cost a fraction of what it would to buy them already finished. Add trim to white hand towels for the bathroom as well.

Shelf Trim

A product called Doily Carte is a 1½-inch-wide shelf trim that looks like a paper doily. One edge is scalloped and the other straight, and it comes in a roll, so you can cut off as much as you need. Apply double-sided Scotch tape to the back of a strip and attach it to the front edge of linen closet shelves. You can order a box of this paper shelf liner from 19 Petticoat Row, 19 Centre St., Nantucket, MA 02554 or it can be purchased from Wolfman-Gold & Good Company in New York City.

Instant Decorator's Trick

Add a strip of shelf trim to the bottom edge of white, sheer bathroom curtains. It's temporary. You can't wash it. But it peels right off the curtain when you're ready to remove it.

Yard Sale
Finds

Yard Sail-ing!

According to my little Oxford Dictionary, the word "sailing" means gliding easily on water by the use of sails. Although I've lived by water all my life, I am more comfortable with two feet planted firmly on land. So I am quite happy with a new kind of sailing that has a different meaning altogether. It is strictly confined to backyards or driveways. As far as I know it has never been practiced offshore, although it is a popular weekend sport in many suburban towns.

"Yard sailing" has everything in its favor. It is the ideal activity for those who love excitement, a challenge, and suspense without effort. There is no talent necessary, no pre-learning period, no advance planning, no preparation, and no major time commitment. Best of all, the cost to get into the game is minimal and everyone wins.

"Yard sailing" is much like a treasure hunt and consists of traveling from one yard to another in search of undiscovered goodies. Each item is a treasure only to the person who finds it. Therefore, this is not considered a competitive sport, except now and then when more than one person spots a desirable item at the same second. But by and large, protocol intervenes and everyone is polite, deferring to the other more often than not. Best of all, if you don't like anything you don't pay. And if the price for something you covet is too high, chances are you can get it lowered by simply asking.

There are two sides to this activity; you can either choose to be a yard sale goer or a yard sale giver, and there are rules for each role.

How to Be a Good Yard Sale Giver

1. The first reason for giving a yard sale is to get rid of things you no longer need or want, so price accordingly. If you really want to end the day with an empty basement, charge ridiculously low prices. This is what attracts people to a yard sale. The two dollars you get for a kitchen chair is a token for the privilege of carting it away. Once it's gone, don't think you should have charged five dollars. Everyone wins when it's two dollars.

2. The reward for cleaning out your basement is that you get paid for the junk rather than having to pay to have it hauled away. Your trash becomes someone else's treasure. Remember this when asked to lower a price. The objective is to be rid of it.

3. Make your yard sale look exciting by having lots of stuff. Never hold a yard sale to get rid of five or six items. This only antagonizes the people who came to hunt for bargains. Spread the stuff out on tables and put price stickers on everything.

4. Clothes and books are best-sellers. Clean clothes and really cheap books sell even better. Books will get people hunting and pecking and create a crowd. The absolute rule is: ten cents for paperbacks, a quarter or fifty cents for hardcovers. Either you want them out of your sight or you don't!

How to Be a Good Yard Saler

1. It's not hard to be a good yard saler. All you need is an open mind. Expect nothing, and be overjoyed when you find a strainer for ten cents that you didn't know you needed.

2. Don't look around and proclaim out loud, "What a lot of junk!" If you don't like what you see, quietly leave and mumble a polite thank-you to the sale giver for taking the trouble to set it up at all.

3. If you see something you want for fifty dollars and think it's worth five, you can do one of two things. Follow the good etiquette rules of haggling and say, "Would you consider less?" The answer will usually be, "Make me an offer." Or you can do the cowardly thing, which is what I usually do. Mutter a thank-you and leave!

4. And finally, do not under any circumstances arrive at 8 A.M. for a yard sale that advertised "10 to 2. Positively no early birds!" It's very bad form.

A few weeks ago my yard saling partner Maddie and I initiated her ten-year-old granddaughter Amanda into the game. Here was a born yard saler. For two dollars she came home with a game of Monopoly, a brand new talking alarm clock, a gold bracelet, two comic books, 100 postcards, stationery, and Nancy Thayer's "Lost Spirit," which she included for me.

All of which goes to prove that one is never too young or too old to enter the sport. And I challenge anyone to come up with a more satisfying two hours' worth of fun for a mere two dollars.

More Yard Sale Know-how

It's 9 A.M. on Saturday morning and everyone with a penchant for finding pearls among swine is making the yard sale rounds. Sooner or later, even those with a modicum of curiosity can't help but stop "for a quick peek" as they drive by the ubiquitous sign announcing such an event.

I've been a yard sale attendee for most of my adult life and I can't pass up even the meagerest display on a rickety card table. I am convinced that any household item I need will eventually turn up at such a sale.

Advice for Yard Salers

The other day I came upon an old book in the library called "The Garage Sale Manual." It intrigued me because the authors approached the subject as an economic experience and managed to fill 224 pages in the process. Rather than as a few hours devoted to the disposal or accumulation of odds and ends, a rather frivolous activity, they described it as a whole psychological experience. Their advice was so humorous as to be worthy of repeating. They offer the following:

1. "Eliminating excess stuff is like weeding a garden, it gives what remains a chance to come alive." I wasn't quite sure what exactly was growing, but I assume this passage refers to the furnishings left in your home.

2. "It's a chance to establish new relationships." I don't know about you, but I find it downright impossible

to create a meaningful relationship based on the dickering of a quarter off an item.

3. And this high-powered economic business advice: "Prepare for the power of bargaining. If something is 35 cents always offer 30 cents!" And to the seller they advise, "When offered less always hesitate before accepting the offer. This will make the buyer think twice before doing it a second time."

Sellers Beware!

The prize-winning chapter strongly advises being on the alert for the early bird and "rich biddy" who are both pesky specimens, demanding attention in handling. And how do you spot these pesky specimens? "They drive Mercedes and wear suede jackets," say the authors about the "rich biddies." The early birds, warn the authors, come before 9 A.M. and tell you they have to be at work so they thought they could have a peek before everyone else arrives. The authors caution that this is a ploy used over and over again to get the really good and valuable "stuff."

Just Plain Fun

So much for the advice from the so-called experts. If you haven't gone to a yard sale, it's lots of fun for everyone who loves the element of surprise, getting a bargain, and finding something you didn't know you absolutely needed. It doesn't take much time, it's a cheap form of entertainment, and it can often yield a treasure for a pittance.

If you haven't given a yard sale, it's a great way to clean out your unwanteds, make a little money, and meet your neighbors (maybe this is the relationship part of the book), and it gives you a chance to hone your business skills (the bargaining part of the book). As for rubbing elbows with the "rich and famous," I haven't found them hovering around card tables in backyards yet, but I'm ever hopeful they'll show up at my next sale.

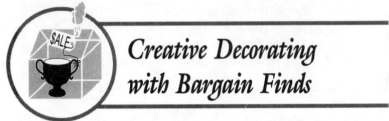

Creative Decorating with Bargain Finds

Yard sales offer a terrific opportunity to find some real treasures from other people's discards. Sometimes finding the unusual can dictate a decorating direction.

Chinaware

It's easy to find chinaware at yard sales. This might encourage you to create an interesting table with mismatched items. Finding one piece can lead to a collection of others. I always look for white dishes.

One-of-a-Kind Finds

Approach the yard sales with an open mind. You never know what you'll find. I didn't know I needed the cute little rosebud teapot until I saw it, or the Roseville planter that was a real bargain, even if it was in pieces. (I was able to glue it together and it looks great in my garden.) Was I looking for such an item? Not on your life! But that's the fun of bargain decorating...to be able to spot a gem and, if need be, evaluate, on the spot, how fixable it is.

Getting Just What You Want

A friend of mine was looking for a round table to comfortably accommodate four with enough room to seat six when needed. Sometimes you have to be creative to achieve the goal. For example, at one sale we came upon a wonderful plant pedestal. At another we found a small, round metal table, large enough for four, but never six. Either of these items could do the trick with a little ingenuity.

For the first, a plywood top could be cut to the desired size and mounted onto the plant pedestal. The plywood could be covered with a floor-length tablecloth.

The smaller table needed a coat of paint. Easy enough. The size, however, would never accommodate six people. This is an easy problem to solve with a table extender, a thin but sturdy board made of composition material that is placed on top of the table. It comes in various round sizes and folds in the center for easy storage. It's a common item sold through mail order catalogs and home accessory stores. A table covering is needed, but what a simple way to solve this particular problem.

Quick Tips

Home Maintenance Tips

Good home design starts with good home maintenance. Decorative painting is fine, but a sticky dresser drawer needs attention first.

Worn Drawers

After years of use, the bottom rails of wood drawers sometimes wear grooves in the front cross-members of dressers. Fill the grooves with Plastic Wood to create a strong, wear-resistant surface. Then sand the area so it is smooth and finish with a coating of wax. The drawer will fit well and operate smoothly.

Socket Sense

One drop of oil on the thread of a light bulb will prevent corrosion between the socket and bulb. This is especially effective for outdoor fixtures.

Squeaky Madness

Are squeaky doors driving you mad? Here's a simple remedy. Cut a ½-inch-diameter circle of felt and punch a hole in the middle to form a felt washer. Put this under the top of the pin on the door hinge and saturate with oil. It will be squeaky-free for years. If oil gets sticky, a few drops of alcohol will soften it. Squeaky floors can be silenced from the surface by lubricating the board edges with oil. Be sure to wipe surface clean.

For a free booklet of household tips, write to: "Secrets," P.O. Box 561, Gibbston, NJ 08027.

Fine Furniture Finish

For a superfine finish on newly stained or varnished furniture, dip a small piece of fine black sandpaper into warm, soapy water and rub lightly over the surface. Keep it wet as you work. Wipe away all residue before applying clear furniture paste wax.

Painting Around Hinges

When painting anything with a hinge attached, such as kitchen cabinets, coat the hinges with rubber cement. When the paint is dry, rub the rubber cement off the hinges with your fingers or a gum eraser.

Sanding in Tough Places

To sand chair rails or other curved areas before painting, place a strip of 3M adhesive-backed sandpaper on the palm of your hand and rub back and forth.

Wobble Away

Glue a button to the bottom of a wobbly chair or table leg.

Painting Tight Corners

To get paint into tight corners, cut the paint brush bristles into a V shape.

Tips for Buying a Mattress

You've decided it's time to redecorate your bedroom. The fun part is picking out the fabric, wallpaper, carpets, and furniture. But the most important item to consider before all else is your mattress. It's not the most exciting purchase, but it's the one that stands between you and a good night's rest, which adds up to happier, more stress-free days. The following are some tips from the folks who make mattresses.

Togetherness

Unless you sleep alone, shop with your significant other. One of you may like to sink into slumber up to your armpits while the other may like to keep a stiff upper lip. Compromise might be in order.

Try It Out

Wear comfortable clothes so you won't feel awkward lying down and tossing about. Take time to do this even if you feel as though you're making a spectacle of yourself. An extra minute might mean many nights in splendor.

See It in Writing

Check the warranty and get the guarantee against defects in writing. I'm always tempted to pull that tag off, the one with the big warning about being arrested if you do so. My natural instinct is to pull it off in defiance. Don't. That tag is an insurance policy. It's your only hedge against a defect should you have to return the mattress for any reason.

Splurge

This is not the time or place to save money. Scrimp elsewhere. This mattress should last a long, long time. It's a big purchase. I bought a terrific mattress and box spring many years ago and not a night goes by that I don't sigh as I climb into bed and say, "I love this bed." At the end of a really trying day I actually savor the thought of getting into that bed. The problem is I have trouble getting out of it as well!

Mattress Care

There are some things to know about caring for your mattress.

1. Rotate it regularly. This means turning it over and around so the foot is at the head. It will wear more evenly.
2. Handles are for positioning, not for lifting. The Beauty Rest people say you can actually harm the insides of your mattress by pulling on the handles.
3. Save tags! Need I say more?
4. Vacuum your mattress occasionally, as you vacuum upholstery.
5. Use a good quilted bed pad to protect the mattress and cushion your body. A thick, fitted bed pad combined with really fine sheets makes for a sensational night's sleep. When you buy new sheets, wash them and use fabric softener before putting them on the bed for the first time. I find that even expensive sheets are never as soft as old ones that have been washed a zillion times.
6. Boards are not for bodies. If you don't have enough support you need a new mattress.

For a free booklet on "How to Buy a Mattress," write to: Healthful Sleep, P.O. Box 95465, Dept. C191, Atlanta, GA 30347. I don't know about you, but I love getting these little helpful booklets. If the information isn't relevant at the moment, I file the booklet away for a time when I might need it. If you don't need a new mattress now, sooner or later you'll be considering it. A good mattress should last for about ten years.

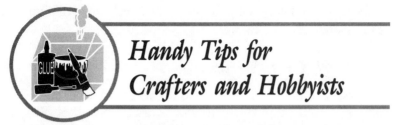

Handy Tips for Crafters and Hobbyists

Every time I discover a handy crafting tip I save it in my "good idea" file. Here are a few that I think are worth knowing about.

Sewing Breeze

Rub a piece of fabric softener sheet over your needle and thread to make quilting a breeze. The slick needle will go through layers of material with ease.

Take a Load Off

When doing hand sewing, place a fat pillow in your lap to take the strain off your shoulders. If you quilt on a frame, put the pillow on your knee to rest your elbow.

Recycling Trick

For those who like to design and cut your own stencils, save the clear plastic lids from tops of stationery boxes. They are perfect for cutting out small designs. The acetate is also excellent for making patchwork and appliqué templates.

Perfect Stitches

To sew perfectly straight seams, place a strip of masking tape on the fabric and stitch along the edge. Peel tape away when finished.

Spray Painting Small Items

When spray painting a small item on all sides, place it on a paper-covered lazy susan. Spin with one hand while you spray paint with the other.

Quick Cross-Stitch

Use a gingham fabric for the background. A charted design can be copied square for square onto the fabric squares, which are larger than even-weave Aida cloth. Gingham comes in different sizes and colors.

Non-Slip Quilt Templates

Use sandpaper to cut quilt templates. Draw the pattern on the smooth paper side and place the sandpaper face down on the fabric. It won't slide.

Keeping Pins Sharp

Shavings from a pencil sharpener are terrific for filling a pincushion and will keep the pins sharpened. Sand-filled cushions work well too.

Easy Paint Touchups

Need to touch up something with a dab of paint? Use a cotton swab rather than buying or dirtying a paint brush. These are also great for children's painting.

Storing Yarn

If you do any knitting or crochet work, store the yarn in a clear plastic hanging closet bag with shelves and a zipper front.

Shortcut Decorating Savvy

Everyone wants to get things done more quickly, more easily, or better. The following shortcuts should help.

Arranging Dried Flowers

When working with dried flowers, spray with hair spray to keep brittle leaves and petals from shedding.

Quick Pillow Covers

Large napkins or handkerchiefs can be stitched together for inexpensive and good-looking throw pillow covers.

Plate Display

Do you have plates too pretty to store out of sight? Display them on narrow shelves. First attach slim wood slats across the bottom edge of the shelves to keep the plates from slipping.

Silk Sensations

Turn pretty silk scarves into decorative throw pillows. Choose brightly colored, big floral patterns. Stitch two together and you've got elegant pizzazz for a sofa or bed.

Summer Pleasure All Year Long

Wash and bleach scallop shells and attach them in a row along a chair rail, or line them along the top of a door molding.

Quick Ties

Tie back curtains with silk braided tassels sold in fabric or upholstery shops. The Laura Ashley mail order catalog offers an extensive and beautiful variety to choose from.

Jazz Up the Bathroom

Pay attention to the bathroom by adding a fresh plant, lace curtains, and a pretty tray full of bath oils and magazines within easy reach of the tub. Fluffy new towels will give the room a lift for the least amount of effort and cost. Use a sheet in a matching color to make a new shower curtain.

Rice On

Rice-paper shades let in light but afford privacy. They're easy to install and are carefree. This will give a bathroom or bedroom a clean, fresh look.

Tabletop Cover-up

If you've been using placemats on your dining table, switch to a floor-length tablecloth, or cover the table with a quilt. It will make your mealtimes more interesting.

Natural Tiebacks

Dress up your curtains with small wreath tiebacks. Make or buy vine wreaths and add your own decorations.

Instant Curtains

Use a set of pillowcases with a border trim for café curtains. Attach the closed edge to a rod with clip-on rings. Open the seam of a third pillowcase so that it is wide enough to use as a valance.

New Use for Placemats

Use two round, quilted placemats to make a pillow cushion for a rocking chair. Stitch them together leaving 2 or 3 inches open for stuffing. Fill with quilt batting or foam and stitch opening closed. Some placemats even come with a ruffle all around.

Fall Arrangement

For a quick country arrangement, fill a basket with fresh vegetables and herbs.

Mirror, Mirror, on the Wall

Group mirrors of various sizes and shapes into a pattern as you would with paintings. If you have interesting antique frames you can easily have mirrors cut to fit them. This creates a fascinating effect in a room.

Quick Candleholders

For a quick, free centerpiece on the patio table, use empty glass baby-food jars to hold votive candles. Decorate them with grape leaves tied with twine and group them together.

Family and Friend

Add a little spice to the family lineage. Arrange different pictures of family members on a blank sheet of paper, then cut a picture of a famous person from a magazine and add the picture to the group. Have the paste-up photo copied and frame.

Bed to Bench

Turn a wooden single bed frame into an elegant bench. Cut the footboard in half, then secure each piece to the sides of the headboard to make the side pieces of the bench. Cut the seat from the bed slats and give the whole thing a slick coat of white paint. Add a cushion or blue and white pillows.

Kids' Tips

Easy shortcuts and quick tips are especially helpful when you have children. Here are a few that might apply to your household needs.

Rainy-Day Smarts

Place a shoe rack by the back door. When the kids come in with wet feet they can remove their shoes and place them on the rack to dry. This is a great way to dry mittens as well.

Shower Gift

For an inexpensive baby shower or wedding gift, buy a picture frame with mats cut for several photos in one frame. Put stickers, pressed flowers, vital statistics, dates, etc. in each cutout area.

Round Up the Zoo

When your child is bored with his or her stuffed animals, try this storage tip. Attach a fishnet to the ceiling so it is tacked loosely all around and fill with the toys. The menagerie will create visual interest.

Keep Baby Safe

If you have a baby coming to visit or you're taking baby to a friend's house, here's an instant safeguard for keeping little fingers out of cabinets. Tie colorful bandannas through the handles and tie the ends in a fat knot. This will temporarily do the trick.

Quick and Easy Headboard

Make an inexpensive headboard for a teenager's bed with a section of picket fence. Paint and secure to the wall behind the bed.

Just for Baby

Make a bassinet skirt from two pairs of tier curtains. Sew them together at the side seams and run a piece of elastic through the heading. Then fit the skirt around the bassinet and stitch to the lining.

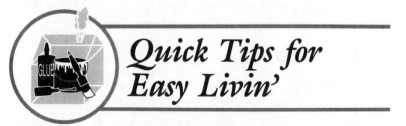

Quick Tips for Easy Livin'

From time to time well-meaning friends and relatives call me with "great tips." Sometimes they're terrific and worth passing along. Other times my "tipsters" forget that I'm writing about home design and the tips run the gamut from cleaning out the garbage can to icing a cake. The following are good tips for quick home design, and if you want to know how to keep ice-cream cones from leaking, you'll find this tip from my mother at the end.

For the Bathroom

Use long wooden dowels on one bathroom wall for holding drying towels.

Bag It

My artist friend Donn Russell offers this tip. Save paper bags efficiently and make it easy to take one at a time from the pile. Fold the bottom portion up so it's flat and smooth, then fold the top with the open end down, so that it fits under the folded-up bottom edge; then smooth down. It will lie flat and compact on a pile and when you need a bag you can lift one off rather than fumbling with a whole pile. Donn uses the bags he saves to make paper roses for ecological gift-box decorations.

Quick Kindling

Save newspapers to make fireplace logs. Roll up a few sheets and tie in a knot. It makes great kindling.

Not for Knitting Alone

My friend Rosie uses scraps of colorful acrylic yarn to tie roses to her trellises. It won't break in a strong wind and if you use a green color it will blend in with the environment. For colorful basket handles braid different colors of yarn together and attach to each side.

The Clearer to See By

To keep the bathroom mirror from steaming up, wipe a thin coat of shaving cream on the mirror, then buff with a soft cloth.

Unstick Labels

Use nail polish remover to get the sticky labels off glass, pottery, or plastic items. Pour directly on the label, then rub off with a clean cloth or paper towel.

Sifting Soil

Use an old flour sifter to spread a light layer of earth over newly planted seeds.

Not for Pots Alone

A long pot holder with a pocket at each end is perfect for holding reading glasses, a pad and pencil, or sewing or crafting items over the arm of a chair.

Sachet Sense

Save your scented candles to make sweet-smelling sachets. Chop the candles into small pieces and place in a bag. Tie with a pretty ribbon.

Sweet Scents

And here's another idea for making sweet-scented sachets for inside your drawers or linen closet. Take used fabric softener sheets that go in the dryer and with pinking shears cut them into fourths. Put a teaspoon of potpourri in the center of each square, gather up the ends, and tie with a thin ribbon. The scent comes through.

Lining Shelves

When covering a shelf with self-adhesive paper, use a rolling pin to remove bubbles. Start in the center and roll toward the outer edges. A yardstick on edge also does the trick. Glide it over the paper as you apply pressure. To remove bubbles after the paper is down, prick with a pin and pat back into place.

Wash 'n' Wear

Mount a closet pole over a washer and dryer to hang just-dried shirts and keep them wrinkle free. Store laundry aids in a pretty basket next to the washer. It will boost morale and make you feel organized.

Short on Space

Roll up towels and place them on end in a large basket that can sit on the floor under the sink or next to the tub.

Save the Drips

Even though it has nothing to do with home design, who can justify leaving out a tip from one's mother? So here's my mother Ruth Linsley's tip for keeping homemade ice-cream cones from dripping: Place a marshmallow in the bottom of the cone before inserting the scoop. The marshmallow acts as a stopper so the ice cream doesn't ooze out the bottom of the cone. My mother says she can't wait to finish the ice cream so she can get to the marshmallow. Some mothers never grow up!